GREEN GUIDES
Compost

This is a **FLAME TREE** book
First published in 2009

Publisher and Creative Director: Nick Wells
Project Editor: Victoria Lyle
Art Director: Mike Spender
Layout Design: Theresa Maynard
Digital Design and Production: Chris Herbert
Picture Research: Victoria Lyle
Proofreader and Indexer: Amanda Leigh

Special thanks to: Chris Herbert, Rebecca Kidd, Polly Prior, Sam Shore

The author wishes to thank: Richard for being the rock beneath my feet and the wind beneath my wings.
Verona for your patience, understanding and love. Peace for teaching me to appreciate nature in a different way.
Peggy for your enthusiasm and encouragement. Russell for presenting fulfilling opportunities.

11 13 12 10
5 7 9 10 8 6 4

This edition first published 2009 by
FLAME TREE PUBLISHING
Crabtree Hall, Crabtree Lane
Fulham, London SW6 6TY
United Kingdom

www.flametreepublishing.com

Flame Tree Publishing is part of The Foundry Creative Media Co. Ltd

ISBN 978-1-84786-531-1

A CIP record for this book is available from the British Library upon request.

The author has made all reasonable efforts to ensure that the information in this book is correct at the time of going to print, and the publishers cannot accept any liability for incorrect or out-of-date information. The publisher would be glad to rectify any omissions in future editions of this book.

Printed in China

Pictures courtesy of Clean Air Gardening (www.cleanairgardening.com): 105; **ComposTumbler** (www.compostumbler.com): 114; **fotolia** and Paul Hebditch: 226; photoconcepts1: 59, 48; **Green Cone Limited** (www.greencone.com): 147, 151, 233; **iStock** and Maxwell Attenborough: 115; AtWaG: 110; audaxl: 131; Kjell Brynildsen: 132; Oliver Childs: 241; Sebastien Cote: 17, 101, 201, 231; Phil Danze: 13; Lydia Dotto: 12, 103; Paul Erickson: 221; Lisa Fletcher: 138; Ian Francis: 149; Peter Garbet: 65; gremlin: 153; Loretta Hostettler: 119; kkgas: 161; Graham Klotz: 181; Dennis Oblander: 80; Purdue9394: 123; Ashleigh Quinn: 99; RMAX: 117; Solidago: 164; Paul Vasarhelyi: 211; Vincent Voigt: 73; Julee Wyld: 126; **Just Green** (www.just-green.com): 113, 135, 136; **Recycleworks** (www.recycleworks.co.uk): 107, 129, 156; **Shutterstock** and Angelaoblak: 24; Mircea Bezergheanu: 50; Vera Bogaerts: 81; cen: 21; Chrislofoto: 78; chudoba: 15; Colette3: 224; Neale Cousland: 66; Steve Cukrov: 48; Sharon Day: 62, 193; Brad Denoon: 95; Elena Elisseeva: 170, 174; Christopher Elwell: 196; Joan Ramon Mendo Escoda: 68; Farferros: 247; Brian Finestone: 54; Kurt G: 222; Nicola Gavin: 182; Joe Gough: 85; Robert Grubba: 121; Lijuan Guo: 167; Anthony Harris: 70, 188; Alex Hinds: 47; David Huntley: 30; Inc: 3, 32; Maciej Karcz: 19; John Kershner: 205; Sharon Kingston: 28, 39, 186; Anne Kitzman: 171; Vadim Kozlovsky: 22; Scott Latham: 234; Leshik: 208; letty17: 189; LockStockBob: 216; Lonni: 11; Tomas Loutocky: 202; Liane M: 198; Victor I. Makhankov: 83; Jason Maehl: 145; mates: 93, 185; Monika23: 41; MY_NEW_ IMAGES: 130; Andrei Nekrassov: 122; Zavodskov Anatoliy Nikolaevich: 45; Rafal Olechowski: 143; Slyadnyev Oleksandr: 175; Pakhnyushcha: 77; pirita: 206; Aleksej Polakov: 218; Dr Morley Read: 26; Stephen Aaron Rees: 169; Francesco Ridolfi: 166; Eduardo Rivero: 236; Benedikt Saxler: 238; Gordana Sermek: 163; silabob: 74; Egidijus Skiparis: 91; slowfish: 173; Smit: 87; Carolina K. Smith, M.D.: 195; Stephen Snyder: 213; Margaret M. Stewart: 37, 229; Nicholas Sutcliffe: 31; teekaygee: 96; TheSupe87: 42; Svetlana Turilova: 217; Graca Victoria: 230; Whitechild: 214; Jerome Whittingham: 61; Feng Yu: 88; **Wormcity** (www.wormcity.co.uk): 137, 155.

GREEN GUIDES
Compost

RACHELLE STRAUSS

Foreword by HEATHER GORRINGE of *Wiggly Wigglers*

FLAME TREE
PUBLISHING

Contents

It is estimated that around 60 per cent of household waste is compostable. By putting your vegetable peelings and garden clippings on the compost heap instead of in the bin you will drastically reduce your waste and nature will recycle it into free food for your soil. Composting is great exercise and getting outside is good for your physical and mental wellbeing. Of course, it is also fun... so what are you waiting for?

Listed in alphabetical order, this chapter provides a comprehensive list of what you can and can't compost. Whereas some may be obvious, others may come as a surprise. For example, did you know that chicken and pigeon faeces are excellent additions to the compost pile? Including tips on how to treat and what to include with each ingredient, this is a chapter to refer to again and again.

How to Compost 58

Taking you step-by-step through the composting process, this chapter covers the carbon:nitrogen ratio, the mix of greens and browns and how to layer your pile. It describes hot and cold composting methods and the importance of aeration, temperature and moisture to the heap. Finally, it gives an indication of how long it will take to produce compost and its appearance, texture and smell when fully cured.

Compost Bins & Composting Systems . . . 98

This chapter describes the numerous compost bins available, from standard moulded plastic bins to tumbling composters and open heaps. The pros and cons of each are put forward so that you can decide which is best suited to you. Whether you have a large or small garden and no matter how much time or money you have, there is a compost bin for you.

Other Types of Composting 134

This chapter addresses other types of composting. Wormeries and bokashi bins, allow you to process organic waste, even if you have no garden, and Green Cones and Green Johannas enable you to dispose of cooked food waste, including meat, fish and bones. Or how about making leaf mould? This is an alternative to composting in the autumn, when you may have a surplus of leaves.

Using Compost 160

Compost can be used in many ways and in a variety of places. This chapter explains how compost can be used as a soil improver, as mulch, as potting compost and to maintain lawns, amongst other things. As soon as you start using compost you will realize that you can never have enough!

The Composting Year 180

This chapter explains what you should be doing to your compost pile and with your compost throughout the year. From using compost to plant seeds in spring, adding grass clippings to the pile in summer and fallen leaves in autumn, to insulating your bin in winter, this chapter is a detailed guide to the composting year.

Composting Problems & Solutions 220

If things are not going well with your compost pile then this chapter can help. Whether you have unwanted visitors, such as wasps or rats, or your heap does not seem to be doing anything, there is a solution. Organized alphabetically for easy reference this chapter will sort out your composting problems in no time.

Foreword

Whilst recycling your waste is certainly better than it ending up in landfill, composting at home is one of the best ways to make a difference to the environment and reduce your carbon footprint.

Around 60 per cent of household waste is compostable; by composting this at home instead of sending it to landfill you avoid transporting the waste to the landfill, prevent dangerous greenhouses gases from being released as the food decomposes and do not need to buy compost, which can be made from endangered peat bogs.

However, here's the clincher, by composting at home you end up with free compost for use in your own garden made out of a pile of rubbish! Now that beats the bottle bank any day – although don't let me put you off that one!

There has been a tendency in the past to think of composting as a sort of 'black art', where expert horticulturalists hold a secret recipe of ingredients, mixing and cooking, which is then passed down to the next generation through a whisper and a nod of the head in the potting shed.

This book successfully demystifies the whole process and encourages us to just 'get on with it', garden or not. There is a full explanation of what equipment you can use and why, but the tone is down to earth (excuse the pun) and Rachelle Strauss speaks from experience, having 'got on with it' herself!

I have been enthusiastically composting for the past 20 years and encouraging others to do the same. I've found it particularly satisfying to see how my soil has changed – it is now teeming with earthworms and living organisms. In turn, this has inspired a veggie patch that provides some delicious suppers.

I've noticed that those who compost at home seem to produce less waste in the first place. I'm not sure whether that is because they are more aware of the problem of disposing of waste, or simply because they have to deal with it themselves. Whatever the reason, home composting is surely a win-win for our environment, the planet and us.

Happy Composting!

Heather Gorringe CEO, *Wiggly Wigglers*

Introduction

Have you ever wondered what that lovely, sweet-smelling, crumbly stuff that you buy in plastic bags from the garden centre each spring is? You part with your money, get your goodies home and fill your pots or cover your flowerbeds with the contents of these bags; but what is compost?

It's a Natural Process

Imagine if every leaf that fell from your trees, all your grass clippings, every dead plant or rotting vegetable stayed where they fell and didn't break down. We'd be in a bit of a mess by now wouldn't we? We would be living on a planet covered with mountains of leaves, twigs, rotting food and grass clippings, not to mention other things!

Compost Happens!

Fortunately, the natural process of decomposition happens all the time. In spring, plants grow abundantly and in autumn most die back. Leaves fall off the trees and eventually they decompose. Everything that lives eventually dies and falls into the soil to be recycled into new life. We don't need to control it, it happens automatically. Given enough time, all biodegradable material will decompose and produce compost. Hence the saying 'compost happens!'

What's In the Bag?

That stuff that you buy in plastic bags with compost written on the side is simply broken-down, organic material. Organic matter only becomes compost after it has thoroughly decomposed. This enables the compost to release nutrients into the soil, which is the primary function of adding compost to your garden. Whatever soil type you have, it will benefit from a good helping of organic material in the form of compost.

What is Home Composting?

When you actively compost, by using a compost heap or similar, you help speed up the natural decomposition process by adding favourable conditions such as moisture, warmth and air. Nature is wonderful, but can take a long time to decompose things. For example, on the forest floor, wood bark and leaves can take several years to break down completely. In a home-composting system, you can increase the decomposition rate.

Taking a Leaf from Nature's Book

Composting can be done at home in the smallest of gardens. Many years ago, the only fertilizers farmers and gardeners had were compost and animal manure. Since the industrial revolution we have relied heavily on chemical soil additives. However, with a heightened awareness of environmental issues, people are discovering once again that recycling organic waste into compost is a natural and healthy way to improve the soil and reduce landfill waste. Not only does it quite literally turn 'trash' into 'treasure', but it utilizes natural processes instead of relying on machinery and chemicals.

From Trash to Treasure

Consider the wonderful cycle of composting. You fill up your bin or composting area with rotting vegetables, grass clippings or hedge prunings; it all starts to rot down, and within a few months you are the proud owner of beautiful, rich, dark, sweet-smelling and moist compost! It no longer bears much resemblance to the original ingredients. Have you ever wondered what is happening in that mysterious compost bin of yours?

Have You Thought Of?
Consider for a moment the wonderful cycle of composting – everything that grows in the soil, eventually dies and releases nutrients for new growth.

Put organic waste into your compost bin.

Ensure you have a good mix of greens and browns.

Nature, aided by microorganisms, decomposes your waste.

Use your compost to improve your soil and grow flowers, fruit and vegetables.

After about a year your compost will be ready.

What Happens In My Compost Bin?

During the composting process, each item of organic waste breaks down. This is done by organisms, from tiny single-cell bacteria to large, wiggly earthworms, who dutifully munch their way through the materials in your compost bin several times. Each time they are eaten, the components of these materials are gradually altered, so that they become unrecognisable. Compost is a living ecosystem; full of microbes, healthy bacteria and nutrients. The decomposition of raw materials is performed by a vast range of bacteria, yeast, fungi, insects and worms.

Food, Glorious Food

Enhanced soil fertility and improved soil health are two of the benefits compost can have when incorporated in your garden. Compost varies wildly in physical characteristics and texture depending on the original ingredients. Some compost is drier than others, some has more fibrous materials, and others are darker. It all depends on the original materials and the type of composting you choose. Essentially though, you are creating the perfect food for your soil.

About This Book

In this book you will learn all you need to know about successful home composting. If you've been put off in the past due to composting 'failures' then this book can help. Once you've learned a few tricks and put some new habits in place, you'll be composting like a pro and your compost will bring gasps of delight and envy from your friends.

What You Will Learn

Not only will you find out why composting is a simple, rewarding and ecological activity, you'll learn all you ever wanted to know about successful and nutrient-rich compost. This is a user-friendly guide written in simple language that will help you to create rich, nutritious food for your soil.

Find Out

- What **can and cannot** go into your compost heap and why.
- What to **do with** your compost once you have made it.
- How to home compost with **limited time and space**.
- **When to start** your compost heap and how to add new ingredients.
- What you should do to your compost heap throughout the **gardening year**.
- How to **reduce** your risk of fruit flies, wasps, rats and other horrors.
- How to **prevent** your compost heap turning into a slimy, green mess.

Composting Through the Seasons

A compost bin isn't just for fair weather gardening. Throughout the year you can be taking active steps towards creating the perfect compost for your soil.

Spring

During spring your compost bin will start to become more active, so get some air in there to warm up the pile and get things moving. Take any finished compost from your pile and dig it into your soil.

Summer

During the summer you need to feed that hungry bin of yours! It will be most active now, so keep things chopped up small, nice and moist and let the magic happen.

Autumn

Temperatures are dropping, so think about covering your compost to keep things warm and snug. Spread any finished compost on top of your soil and let the worms do their work during the winter.

Winter

Even though you might not produce much garden waste, you can still add your kitchen scraps. If it's particularly cold where you live, you can tuck your compost heap up with straw or hay for the winter.

Why Compost?

Reduces Waste and Protects the Environment

You might be wondering what all the fuss is about with home composting. After all, it's easy to grab a few bags of compost from your local garden centre and who can be bothered to separate compostable stuff from the rest of the household waste after a busy day? In addition, compost can be complicated, it stinks, it gets slimy and flies are attracted to it. Rest assured, there are plenty of good reasons to make your own compost. It's free, can save you money, is good for your garden and the environment. But that's not all...

Reduce, Reuse, Recycle

Most of us understand the importance of reducing, reusing and recycling – 'the Three R's'. Many people are learning to consume less in order to reduce the eventual burden on resources. Some find creative ways to reuse things instead of dumping them. Organizations such as www.freecycle.org help pass on unwanted goods for free to those who might need them. Many of us separate our recyclable items for kerbside collections or make frequent visits to local recycling centres.

Trashy Treasure

Composting is the ultimate act of recycling. In the UK, every person produces about half a tonne of waste per year. Collectively, that amounts to 30 million tonnes. It is estimated

Tip

Join www.freecycle.org and give your unwanted items a new home.

that around 60 per cent of household waste is compostable; materials such as paper and cardboard, some textiles, wood, garden waste and kitchen peelings can be recycled on the compost heap, yet regularly end up in the landfill. Recycling these items into compost turns 'trash' into 'treasure'.

The Three R's

Composting satisfies all three R's by reducing the amount of compost you need to buy from garden centres. Home composting is a wonderful way to reuse items that might otherwise end up in the landfill by using them to feed your compost pile instead. And finally, home composting shows us how to recycle useful products into something valuable for our soil.

Have You Thought Of?

**Around 40 per cent of methane gas is produced by landfill.
What could you do to reduce the amount of landfill waste you create?**

Climate Change

Many people think that throwing their vegetable peelings, garden clippings and waste paper into the bin is okay because it all decomposes once it reaches the landfill. Unfortunately this is not true – not much magically disappears in the landfill. Adding compostable materials to the landfill can, in fact, cause big problems that contribute to climate change.

Methane

Organic materials such as paper, leaves and vegetable peelings need air and water to decompose fully. When compostable materials enter the landfill, air cannot get to them so they decompose anaerobically. This produces methane. Methane is reported to be 20 times more potent than carbon dioxide, making it a harmful greenhouse gas. Reducing the amount of compostable materials you send to landfill reduces the amount of methane produced and helps in the fight against global warming.

Got a Bad Case of Gas? Then Compost!

According to the Environment Protection Agency, the largest methane emissions come from the decomposition of waste in landfills, which accounts for 34 per cent of all methane emissions in the US. Similarly in the UK, according to the Department for Environment, Food and Rural Affairs (Defra), 40 per cent of methane gas is produced by landfill. When you compost, oxygen helps the waste to decompose aerobically, which produces carbon dioxide, but not methane. So composting can greatly reduce the amount of greenhouse gas generated and emitted. According to the Waste and Resources Action Programme (WRAP) in the UK, composting at home for just one year can save global warming gases equivalent to all the CO_2 your kettle produces annually.

Reduces Your Carbon Footprint

If your compostable waste is picked up at the kerbside, how does it get to the landfill site? That's right – big lorries, requiring a lot of fuel, come to your home and take your things to that magical place called 'away'. In addition, some of your vegetable peelings may have come from fruit and vegetables that have travelled from the other side of the world to get to your kitchen.

Food Miles

Every time we buy fruit and vegetables that have been imported, we contribute to global warming. Consider how many miles a banana from Costa Rica has to travel to reach you, compared to an apple plucked from a tree in your garden or from your local farm shop. The difference is huge! If we then take the peelings from these foods and put them in the landfill, they continue to contribute to global warming.

Simple Steps to Reduce Your Impact on the Environment

If you take the peelings and other waste from these foods and turn them into nourishing compost for your soil then you are taking a great step towards reducing your carbon footprint. You're putting fewer things into the landfill, which means less fuel needed to transport your waste. You're not travelling to a garden centre to buy compost wrapped in plastic bags. And you might even be inspired to grow some of your own fruit and vegetables, which will dramatically reduce your food miles.

Reduces Plastic Waste

It is estimated that between 500 billion to a trillion different types of plastic bag are used around the world every year. This amounts to a shocking 1 million bags every minute. Most compost bought from garden centres comes in large, thick plastic bags. Most plastic bags are not made from recycled or renewable materials; they are made from oil, which is a non-renewable resource. Many of these bags are not recyclable and once you've ripped them open to use their contents, they are useless and end up in the landfill.

Plastic Hangs Around

Once plastic enters the landfill, it can take hundreds of years to break down. Plastics are virtually everywhere in modern life. We drink out of them, wrap our food in them, sit on them, drive in them and electronic goods arrive protected in them. Plastics are convenient, durable, lightweight and cheap but they are virtually indestructible, which is bad news for the environment. By making your own compost you'll reduce the amount of plastic you use.

Plastic is Trash

Diverting compostable landfill waste from your trash can to your compost bin will reduce the amount of plastic bin liners you use. By recycling and composting all that you can, you'll reduce your landfill waste; this means that you won't need to buy as many plastic bin liners. Also, if you aren't putting kitchen peelings into the bin there won't be anything sludgy going in there, so you might not need plastic liners at all. You can reduce your use of plastic, save money and put your bin out less often.

> **Tip**
>
> **An easy way to reduce the amount of plastic you use is to take reusable shopping bags to the supermarket.**

Protect Wildlife

The plastic bags that you buy compost in can take up to 1,000 years to break down. Once these bags begin to break down, tiny slivers of plastic can pose a great threat to marine life and other wildlife. Globally, an estimated one million birds and 100,000 marine mammals and sea turtles die every year from entanglement in, or ingestion of, plastics. A Minke whale stranded on a beach in Normandy was found to have 800 g (2 lb) of plastic bags and packaging within its stomach.

Protects Peat Bogs

For decades gardeners have bought peat-based compost. It is inert, cheap and reliable, which makes it a very attractive product. Peat retains moisture and nutrients well. Blended with fertilizer and mineral particles, peat becomes potting compost. However, organizations such as Greenpeace, Friends of the Earth, the Soil Association and the Royal Society for the Protection of Birds (RSPB) are calling for the protection of peat bogs. Peat bogs are being depleted much faster than they can replenish themselves – it can take centuries for a peat bog to regenerate. This is causing a problem for both the environment and wildlife.

Have You Thought Of?

Do a bin audit! Have a look through your trash and see where you can begin to reduce, reuse and recycle more. See http://myzerowaste.com for help.

Wildlife Habitat

Peat bogs are important and valuable wildlife habitats and home to many species of birds, thousands of rare insects and a wealth of unusual plants. Peat grows in a living bog with plants on the surface such as heather and sphagnum moss. When these plants die, they don't rot away because the ground is waterlogged; instead they form peat. Extracting this peat requires draining the bog, which kills everything off and destroys the habitat.

Environment Issues

Recent studies indicate that the world's largest peat bog, located in Siberia, is thawing for the first time in 11,000 years. If this continues, it could release billions of tonnes of methane into the atmosphere. As previously mentioned, methane is a harmful greenhouse gas that contributes to global warming. In the UK, 94 per cent of the natural peat bogs have been destroyed: it is estimated that 70 per cent of this destruction is due to gardeners buying peat-based products, or buying container plants which are potted in peat-based compost.

Preserve the Peat Bogs

Buying peat-based compost means supporting the destruction of a non-renewable environment that sustains some of our most beautiful plant and animal life. By making your own compost, you are doing far more to protect the environment than you might have thought! When you buy plants from a garden centre that are already potted, ask whether they are in peat-based or peat-free compost.

Free Food For Your Soil

Everyone likes a freebie, and that includes your soil! What better way to create free food than to make your own compost? Once you know the basics, you'll be making a wonderful soil conditioner that will reward you with prize crops, beautiful flowers and house plants and a healthy environment. If you grow vegetables, you'll be giving them the best start in life and your home-made compost will ensure you have a good chance of enjoying tasty fruit and vegetables all year round.

Soil Food

Composting produces nitrogen, potassium and phosphorus, as well as various trace elements. In addition, good quality compost can balance out acid or alkaline soils, making them more neutral. Healthy soil produces healthy plants and good compost is the foundation of successful gardening. Feeding your soil with nutrients helps to prevent soil depletion and can help sick soil to recover. It's like a medicine and a superfood in one!

Healthy Roots and Shoots

Soil provides physical support for plants. If your soil has too much clay or sand, is too acid or alkaline or depleted in minerals then you will be limited in the sort of plants that you can grow. Adding compost to your soil balances the mineral content and improves the texture of the soil, which means that you can enjoy a wider variety of healthy plants, flowers and crops. Compost increases the organic matter in soil, otherwise known as humus. Soils rich in organic matter have a lovely, tilthy texture, which is favourable for most plants and a pleasure to work with.

Water Retention

Plants grow best in soils that retain water. Not too much though, otherwise they can rot. Compost is fantastic for improving the quality and moisture-holding ability of your soil. In clay soil, adding organic matter helps to reduce the clumping effect by improving drainage. Good compost literally gets into the spaces between the particles of soil, which over time creates air spaces, leading to more workable soil. In sandy soil, compost will help your soil retain water. Sandy soils have little water and nutrient retention due to their fine, grainy texture. Adding compost to sandy soil will help to bind the loose particles of soil together so they can retain moisture and nutrients more readily.

Nutrients

Like humans, plants need nutrients to thrive. Every time a plant grows, it feeds from the nutrients in the soil, so you need to put nutrition back into the soil. There are different methods of doing this, but adding compost to your soil is one of the best, and easiest. Adding compost to your soil recycles nutrients back in, promotes the health of your plants and can increase yields of fruit, flowers and vegetables.

Don't Go Out Without Your Coat!

Applying unfinished compost as mulch to the surface of your soil is beneficial too. Mulching protects the soil from weather extremes such as heat, cold and wind. Think of it as a coat for your soil; the mulch takes all the battering from the weather, so your soil doesn't have to. Compost is worked into the soil, whereas mulch is spread *on top* of the soil to protect it. Mulch will eventually rot and be worked into the soil by our friends the wiggly worms to become compost.

As Nature Intended

Nature is an expert decomposer. Every flower, leaf, tree and animal that dies eventually decays into the earth, returning to it the nutrients they have taken from the soil, air and rain throughout their lives. Through composting you can learn how to enhance this process and utilize it for your own gardening needs. Composting is natural and safe, and the best place to put your waste organic matter is in the soil, not in the landfill – just as nature intended!

Co-operation, Not Competition

Co-operation is better than competition, especially in the garden. The forces of nature are strong so it's far better to work with them than against them. You know how grouchy and unhelpful you can get when you're over hungry – it's the same for your garden and plants! We only need to look at a large forest or natural habitat to know that nature can take care of things by growing, dying back and recycling nutrients. All we have to do is learn how it is done and support the process.

It's Nature's Way

Nature never wastes a thing. The forests don't need a landfill and neither do the animals. It's only man who creates so much useless waste. Everything produced in the natural world will naturally decompose and provide nutrients for the earth to promote and sustain new growth. During composting, an intricate balance of feeding and digestion of the raw materials is taking place within a community of living organisms from the tiniest single cell bacteria to large and luscious earthworms. Each has its job to do and by providing optimum conditions we can assist the process.

Good For You

Making compost at home is not only good for your soil and the environment; there are many benefits for you, too. Making compost gets you closer to nature, which research shows can enhance your physical and mental health in many ways. On top of that there is the feel-good factor from doing something creative and good for the environment.

Educational and Fun

What better way to learn about nature than to get outside and watch your rotting peelings turn into beautiful compost? Children love to get hands on and teaching them about the cycle of life and decay can enhance their lives and instil a sense of reverence for nature. But it's not just for kids! Even as an adult you'll be amazed at the wonders of compost. One week you have a pile of rotting stuff in your bin and in a few months it has changed into a rich, nutrient-dense soil enhancer.

Hands on Learning

It's easy to pick up a book or read a website about composting, but there is nothing like getting out there and having a go yourself. There is a saying that goes along the lines of 'I hear and I forget, I see and I remember, I do and I understand.'

Which basically means that you can listen to your friend's advice or read a book, but in order to understand, you need to have a go yourself. For kids, it's a great opportunity to learn about recycling, taking care of the garden, and the link between healthy soil and healthy plants.

Back to Basics

There is always something new to learn about composting, so it's a richly rewarding activity to bring into your life. You're never too old to learn something new and it's never too late to start, so why not have a go? You'll be able to see some of the tiny creatures living in your compost bin and it can help to begin to see these creatures as our helpers – great for those who don't like creepy crawlies! Home composting also teaches us patience, which is no bad thing.

Great Exercise

Walking to the compost area a few times a week, adding water and stirring things around with a fork provides great outdoor exercise. There are no gym fees and you don't need to clad yourself in lycra! With our sedentary lifestyles, any opportunity to get out in the great outdoors should be grabbed with both hands.

Sedentary Lifestyles

The health of many people in the Western world is not at its best. Research shows that our sedentary lifestyle is causing more deaths than smoking. Disease risks linked to physical inactivity include heart disease, high blood pressure and obesity. It is estimated that regular exercise and sensible eating could prevent nearly 85 per cent of diseases, such as cardiovascular disease. Taking care of your garden can provide both exercise and healthy food.

Mental Wellbeing

Nothing beats exercise for getting rid of stress, anxiety or depression. Exercise helps to dissipate all that pent-up energy, which means you are better equipped for dealing with stress in your day-to-day life. Home composting is a wonderful way to introduce a bit of slow and gentle fitness into your routine. From walking down your garden with kitchen peelings, to mixing the contents of your compost heap and digging your finished compost into your soil, you can make this as laid-back or energetic as you wish.

Nature as a Healer

There are studies showing that patients with a view of nature from their hospital beds make a quicker recovery than those without. As a result hospital therapy gardens have been developed in order to help patients get healthier, quicker. In addition, research shows that wellbeing and levels of psychological stress are significantly influenced by our natural surroundings. So what are you waiting for? If you want to improve your health, reduce stress and do something you can feel good about, starting a compost heap might be the answer!

The Best Things In Life are Free

Composting can be a completely free activity. You don't need any special equipment and you'll save money on buying bags of compost. The ingredients to add to your compost heap can be found in your kitchen, around your home and in your garden as by-products of your purchases and meals. Everything can be done for free!

Get It or Borrow It

Many of us are looking for ways to cut down on living expenses and save money. Making your own compost helps you to do both of these. Local Freecycle groups offer unwanted compost bins all the time, so why not sign up and see if you can get one? Alternatively you can make your own compost area from pallets, which are readily available for free. For turning the compost all you need is a fork; you might already have one, be able to borrow one from a neighbour or share one through a Local Exchange Trading Scheme (LETS).

You Have All That You Need

Making your own compost does not involve any special clothing or uniform. There is no competition in your own garden, so wear whatever is comfortable and enjoy the great outdoors. Your compost bin isn't fussy either; it will eat eggshells, tea bags, vegetable peelings, scrap paper and a whole host of other things that you do not need to buy, as you'll have many of them already.

Self-sufficiency

Making your own compost is a great first step to take into the world of self-sufficiency. Living in a sustainable way means that you reduce your use of the earth's natural resources and lessen your impact on the environment. The most common ways of doing this are through using different methods of transportation, energy consumption and diet. Sustainable living involves living in harmony with nature, not taking any more than you need and giving back where you can, so that resources do not become depleted. It helps us to take responsibility for our actions and gives us the opportunity to reflect on how our actions today might influence the environment in the future.

The Wheel of Sustainable Life

A truly self-sufficient person or community will only consume things they produce. Considering this, it is easy to see why home composting is an important part of a self-sufficient lifestyle. Home composting allows you to turn your waste into food – almost literally! Dead plants, kitchen peelings and other compostable household materials become compost, the compost feeds the soil, the soil feeds the plants and the plants feed you. As you prepare the food to eat, you put the peelings, cores and other waste parts into the compost bin and the cycle starts again.

Growing Organic

Making your own compost means you don't have to rely on chemical soil enhancers, fertilizers and additives. You can grow organically and, if you are fortunate enough to have a vegetable plot, you will benefit immensely from this method of growing. Research shows that organic food is not only tastier, but is also healthier and better for the environment. You don't run the risk of accidental poisoning from pesticides, which is important if you have children or pets, and you won't be responsible for harming wildlife.

Depleted Soil

Man has existed for a long time on this planet without the need for chemical additions to the soil. We used to put plant and animal material back into the soil to maintain fertility and we enjoyed good quality food. Intensive farming took over and we thought it best to 'hyper fertilize' the soil in order to produce more and more. We believed more was better, but are now left with depleted soil in many areas of the world. As a result, many of the foods we now eat do not contain the trace elements and minerals they once did.

Healthier food

Making and using your own compost allows you to create richly fertile and nutrient-dense soil. This will result in healthier plants, foods and flowers. According to advocates, organically grown food tastes better and contains more nutrients.

Checklist

✓ Find out what **recycling** is collected from your kerbside and use the service.

✓ Have a think about any items from your **weekly trash** that you could start to do without, reuse or recycle

✓ Think about the amount of **fruit and vegetable peelings** you throw away – you could use them for compost.

✓ Could you **buy local** fruit and vegetables? Find out where your nearest farm shops, box schemes or orchards are and contact them.

✓ Make a goal to buy one less **bag of compost** this year and make your own instead.

✓ Get to **know your soil**; is it acid or alkaline, sandy or clay? If you know what you are dealing with, you can see your progress.

✓ Spend some time in **nature**, taking note of the cycles of life and decay.

✓ Get your **family involved**. Learn together about composting and make it an excuse to spend quality time together.

✓ Borrow a book on **organic gardening** from your library and learn about some of the benefits of an organic lifestyle.

What to Compost

What to Put in Your Compost Heap

When you think of making a compost heap, what do you think of adding to it? Kitchen peelings, grass clippings or a little shredded paper, perhaps? If you remember from the chapter Why Compost?, around 60 per cent of your household waste is compostable. In this section you'll discover over 30 items that you can put in your compost bin. They are listed in alphabetical order, so you'll be able to refer to this section time and time again to check whether or not an item can be added to your compost heap. Some of these might come as quite a surprise!

Supporting Nature's Process

A helpful saying that you might like to keep in mind when composting is: 'anything that once lived can live again in another plant.' In nature, when things die back, they fall into the earth and their nutrients feed the soil; composting reflects the natural process of life and decay. Start thinking about the things your household treats as rubbish and consider whether they could be given new life in your compost bin.

New Jargon

Throughout this chapter, you'll come across the words 'greens' and 'browns', as well as carbon and nitrogen. Don't worry about these for now; you'll learn more about them in the next chapter. Using them in this chapter is simply to get you used to seeing the words so that the next chapter makes sense quicker.

Cardboard

Shredded cardboard is an excellent brown to add to your compost pile. It is useful for layering between wetter greens such as grass clippings or vegetable peelings. If your compost heap is quite dry, then you can dampen the cardboard before adding. This makes it easier to tear into pieces anyway. Regular sources of cardboard include the inners from toilet rolls, egg boxes and cereal boxes.

Chickens and Pigeons

No, you can't add a chicken or a couple of pigeons to your compost pile. However, if you keep chickens or pigeons, then you also have their manure, which is a top-notch activator for your compost heap. Concentrated poultry manure and urine is very high in nitrogen and needs to be mixed with high carbon or brown materials such as sawdust or shredded cardboard. Most chicken houses and pigeon coops have sawdust or straw in them, so the ideal thing to do is put the whole lot into your compost heap when you clear out the coop!

Freebies

Chicken and pigeon faeces are great examples of where you can save money. Specialist garden centres can charge a lot of money for chicken manure pellets. You're paying for convenience because the pellets have been dried and compressed for ease of use. If you don't keep birds yourself, you might have a kind neighbour who will donate the offerings of their feathered friend's rear ends to you, or you could try your luck on www.freecycle.org or LETS.

Tip

If you have access to heaps of coffee grounds, for example, if you work in a coffee shop, then you can add them directly to your soil as mulch.

Coffee Grounds

If you can't function without a cup of coffee in the mornings, then don't let your coffee grounds go to waste! You can add the grounds, complete with the paper coffee filter, to your compost heap. This can provide you with a valuable nitrogen-rich green at times when these are a little scarce, such as during the winter when you no longer have any grass cuttings to add to your heap.

Corks

After you've enjoyed a bottle of your favourite wine, you can add the cork to your compost heap. It is better to chop them up before adding them as they are pretty dense and will take a long time to decompose. Just be aware that many corks now are made from plastic and are not real cork. Only add the real ones.

Eggshells

Eggshells contain valuable nutrients, so are a good addition to your compost heap. Crush them before adding. Eggshells can take a surprising amount of time to break down, so don't worry if you find a few pieces still intact when you use your finished compost.

Feathers

If you've just turned your feather mattress or your feather pillows are shedding, you can add the feathers to your compost bin. Mix the feathers with some greens before adding to the heap. If it's nesting season, then you could put odd feathers in a hedge for birds to take as nesting material.

Flowers and Pot Plants

You can compost flowers and moss used in flower arrangements as well as cut flowers and pot plants. Any dead flowers from your garden are also a good addition to the compost heap and are valuable greens.

Fruit Peelings and Cores

As you might be aware from your own fruit bowl, some fruits decompose very quickly, such as grapes or strawberries. Any fruit peelings, cores, stalks and bruised flesh left over from your kitchen or garden can be added to your compost pile. If you use a juicer, then the pulp can go in there too. If you have a little bit of leftover juice, you can add that to the pile as well.

A Word About Citrus

Too much citrus can make the compost mix over-acidic and put worms off, so go easy on the oranges, grapefruit, limes and lemons. In addition, citrus skins can take a long time to decompose. A few citrus rinds, however, are great for adding to the compost with other browns such as sawdust or shredded leaves. Chop the pieces of citrus peel into small pieces and add with other ingredients to help speed things along.

Garden Waste

Garden waste covers a huge variety of things and some are dealt with individually. For now we can assume that old bedding plants, old vegetable plants and windfall fruit are all great additions to the compost heap. Just make sure you chop the larger items up and add a few at a time mixed with some carbon-rich browns so that the compost pile does not get too slimy.

Grass Clippings

Grass clippings provide a rich source of nutrients and are high in nitrogen. Mixing grass clippings into your compost heap can help raise the temperature to stimulate the composting process. However, too many can make the compost wet and slimy, so it's a balancing act. Don't worry about this; you will soon get the hang of how much to add and when.

Wet or Too Many Grass Clippings

If your grass clippings are particularly wet, it's best to spread them out and let them dry for a couple of days before adding them to your compost heap; dried grass clippings do not have the slime factor of wet ones. If you have too many clippings you can either dry them out and store them for adding to your compost area throughout the year, or learn from nature and allow your clippings to return to the earth exactly where they fall when you mow the grass! Alternatively, set up another compost bin or use them as mulch.

Adding Clippings to the Compost Heap

If your grass is particularly long and the clippings are more than a couple of inches long, it's best not to add them to the compost. Use them as mulch instead. Ideally, you would not add more than a 15 cm (6 in) layer of grass clippings to your compost at once as they pack down densely and restrict airflow. To get around this, you can make a kind of sandwich by layering the clippings with something dry (known as browns) such as shredded cardboard, broken up sticks or paper.

Human Hair and Pet Fur

Hair can be added to your compost heap, along with pets' fur. If you're a hairdresser then you'll have access to lots of hair, so why not keep it and gradually add it to your compost? Hair takes quite a long time to decompose, so only add a little at a time and mix with other ingredients. If the hair is highly chemically treated, then it's best not to use it. There are plenty of other materials to choose from!

Human Urine

If you're out in the garden and need to urinate, then the compost bin is a good place to do it! Human urine is rich in nitrogen and some people insist it activates the composting process. Others say that only male urine is any good, which is probably just as well because it's far easier for a man to urinate in a compost heap! If you think about it, it's an ecological thing to do because it saves the flush water in your toilet.

Leaves

Leaves rotting down in your garden or on the forest floor are a classic example of decomposition. Have you ever found a leaf skeleton in your garden? Magnolia and maple leaves are particularly spectacular. Some leaves are better in the compost bin than others, because different types have different decomposition rates.

Compost or Leaf Mould?

Some gardeners think it is sacrilege to add leaves to a compost heap when they could
be made into leaf mould instead. You'll learn more about leaf mould in the Other Types of
Composting chapter (see page 142). Raking leaves is an activity that many people associate
with autumn. It's a great form of exercise and valuable for your garden. Leaving rotting
leaves on your grass can suffocate it and result in muddy patches.

Leaves in the Compost Pile

Leaves can make a useful addition to the compost pile and if you only get a few, for example if you have a couple of trees overhanging your plot from a neighbour's, then by all means rake them up and add them to your compost heap. As with grass clippings, you need to be careful with leaves because they can clump and starve the compost pile of oxygen. Have some shredded paper, cardboard or small twigs on hand to layer in with the leaves as you add them to the compost.

Nail clippings

Next time you cut your nails, don't throw them in the trash can, put them in your compost bin. The same goes for the claws of your feline friends, if they shed them. If you manicure your nails, however, and use nail polish or have fake nails then don't add them to the heap. Nail polish is full of chemicals that might be toxic to the living organisms munching through your waste and fake nails won't break down as they are usually made from acrylic.

Nettles

Many people despair when they see nettles growing in their garden. However, they are great news when it comes to composting. Nettles act as a natural compost accelerator, which can save you money on buying ready-made products. Nettle leaves are rich in nitrogen and will help your compost along nicely. If you have a patch of nettles then put them to good use by adding them to your compost pile.

Alternatively, Make a Cup of 'Tea'

Another way to use nettles is to make a liquid fertilizer with them. Put some nettle leaves in a bucket and add rainwater at a ratio of one part nettles to 10 parts water. Leave them to rot for two to three weeks; they will smell, but don't be put off! To use your natural fertilizer dilute one part of the nettle 'tea' to 10 parts water and use as a liquid feed on nitrogen-loving plants. The remaining sludge can be added to your compost heap. Does that make you feel better about this invasive 'weed'?

Nut Shells

You've had a party and you're left with bowls of peanut and pistachio shells. Instead of sending them to landfill, you can add them to your compost pile. This is best if the nuts are unsalted, but unless you're running a bar and have access to piles of them, a few parties worth of salted nut shells is unlikely to cause any harm to your compost heap. Nut shells are a good brown and will help to balance other wetter greens such as vegetable peelings and grass cuttings in your compost pile.

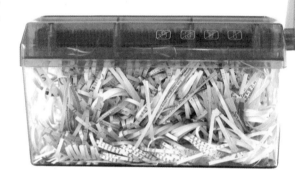

Paper

Like cardboard, paper is a useful brown to add to the compost pile, especially if you predominantly have access to greens like kitchen peelings and grass cuttings. You do need to watch out for certain types of paper and ink, however. Don't use glossy magazines, catalogues and leaflets due to the chemicals in the ink. Regular printer paper, newspaper or old notebooks that you have scribbled in are fine. Many people shred old bank statements, credit card bills and other things that are subject to identity theft and feed them to the compost bin – this makes great use of something you don't want other people getting their hands on!

Have You Thought Of?

Although adding junk mail to your compost is a good way of disposing of it, it's better to stop junk mail being delivered to your home in the first place.

All Sorts of Paper

You probably use lots of different types of paper every day and many of them are great for adding to the compost heap. Newspapers, brown packing paper, used tissues, napkins and kitchen roll, paper bags, paper plates, non waxed food containers and general office paper are all fine. Just remember to shred or tear them up first.

Pet Bedding and Faeces

If you have small, vegetarian pets such as rabbits, guinea pigs or hamsters, then you can add their soiled bedding to the compost heap. Put the whole lot in, complete with the straw, shredded paper or sawdust for a good balance of greens and browns.

Sawdust and Wood Shavings

You might have access to sawdust from pets, a workshop or from chopping wood for a wood burner. Sawdust is very high in carbon and slow to rot, so add a little at a time mixed with other greens such as grass cuttings or vegetable peelings. Ensure that the sawdust or shavings are from untreated, unpainted wood to prevent any toxic chemicals going into your compost bin.

Seaweed and Pondweed

If you have access to fresh seaweed then you can pop it into your compost pile. Seaweed preparations are sold at garden centres, but if you live near the sea you are fortunate enough to be able to benefit from the trace minerals found in fresh seaweed for nothing. Be aware though that seaweed is part of the ecosystem of the shoreline, so don't be greedy. Only take seaweed that has been washed up on the beach; don't start peeling it off rock faces. If you're clearing your garden pond of weeds then these can go into the compost heap too. As with grass cuttings, both seaweed and pondweed will need mixing with some drier browns such as shredded cardboard or scrunched paper.

Slugs and Snails

At last we have a humane way to deal with these pests! Why do we hate them so much? Because they eat our plants! So why not put them to good use?

Into the Compost They Go!

Most people don't want to cause their slimy friends any harm, but neither do they want them eating their prize crops. If you go out with a torch on a midnight mission to collect them up, what on earth do you do with all the critters? Why not dump them in the compost bin and get them to munch through things you don't mind them eating? Co-operation at its best!

Straw and Hay

You can put old straw and hay into the compost bin. They are carbon-rich and quite dry, so make sure you layer them with greens to keep things moist. People who keep small animals such as rabbits and hamsters often have hay and straw to dispose of, so using a compost bin is a good way to keep these ingredients from the landfill.

Tea Bags

If you're a tea drinker, then you'll have tea bags and leaves to add to your compost heap. The only issue with tea bags is that many of them are not made from paper, they are made from polyester which sits around in your compost bin and doesn't break down much. Just rip the bags open and only add the tea leaves.

Textiles

Natural textiles such as cotton, wool and silk can be added to your compost heap. This could be ideal for someone who does a lot of sewing, knitting or crafts and has small scraps of textiles and thread to get rid of. They will need mixing with wetter greens such as kitchen peelings and you should only add a few at a time. If you are unsure about whether your materials have synthetic fibres in them, then play safe and don't add them. Put them in a textiles bank instead.

Used Potting Compost and Soil

Used compost from pots and hanging baskets where the plants have died is ideal for the compost heap. You can also add the contents of grow bags and similar products. Soil can be useful in small quantities as an addition to the compost bin. Too much will make the mixture dense and reduce the airflow, but a little can have beneficial effects such as introducing worms and other micro organisms to a new compost pile.

Vacuum Cleaner Contents and Floor Sweepings

The contents of most vacuum cleaner bags can be added to your compost. However, you need to check a few things first. If you use chemical carpet fresheners or your flooring is not made from natural materials then don't add them. But if you have natural flooring, such as wooden floorboards or wool carpets, and your vacuum cleaner picks up everyday debris, such as dust, pet hair and bits of soil, then it's fine to tip the contents out of the bag into the bin! The same applies to swept wooden floors.

Vegetable Peelings

Any vegetable peelings can go into your compost heap. If you're adding something with a tough woody stem, such as broccoli or cauliflower, then chop it up before putting it in the compost pile. This is not essential, but smaller pieces in your compost bin will rot down faster. Be aware that you might get a few things growing in your compost heap, such as garlic or potatoes. There is nothing wrong with that - it's free food after all, but this might not be where you want things growing!

Have You Thought Of?

Keeping a caddy in the kitchen is the ideal way to store two or three days worth of fruit and vegetable peelings ready for composting.

Wood Ash

If you burn untreated wood on an open fire or wood burner, you'll be left with wood ash. This can be balanced with greens in your compost pile. Wood ash is a good source of potash and is very alkaline. However, some people prefer to put ash directly onto the soil and dig it in, especially if they have very acid soil. If you add it to the compost heap, use very thin layers in between other ingredients.

Recap

You can compost:

- Cardboard
- Chicken and pigeon faeces
- Coffee grounds
- Corks
- Eggshells
- Feathers
- Flowers and pot plants
- Fruit peelings and cores
- Garden waste
- Grass clippings
- Human hair and pet fur
- Human urine
- Leaves
- Nail clippings
- Nettles
- Nut shells
- Paper
- Pet bedding and faeces
- Sawdust and wood shavings
- Seaweed and pondweed
- Slugs and snails
- Straw and hay
- Tea bags
- Textiles
- Used potting compost and soil
- Vacuum cleaner contents and floor sweepings
- Vegetable peelings
- Wood ash

What Not to Put in Your Compost Heap

There are some things, even those given to us by nature, which should not go into your compost bin. Fortunately, you'll notice that this list is much shorter than the previous one.

Biodegradable Nappies (Diapers)

Some brands of nappy (diaper) are sold as biodegradable, but if you start stuffing them in your compost bin, things are likely to come to a grinding halt. If you have just one urine-soaked nappy (diaper) a day, then you might be able to shred it up and add it to the compost heap with some greens, but if the nappy (diaper) is soiled, you shouldn't use it. You would probably need an industrial composting system that is guaranteed to reach high temperatures to decompose the amount of nappies (diapers) used by the average baby. Try washable nappies (diapers) as an ecofriendly alternative.

Cat and Dog Faeces

If you use a wood- or paper-based cat litter then the urine-soaked litter can be gradually added to your compost heap as a brown, mixed in with plenty of other greens. However, the faeces will have to be taken out and disposed of separately. Don't add clay litter to a compost heap. Some people have a completely separate pile just for used cat litter, complete with poop, which they leave to decompose and then use around non-edible plants. This is only any good if you have enough space to dedicate to it. If you have a dog, do not put their faeces into your compost heap either.

Coal Ash

Ashes from coal are not a good addition to the compost heap. Coal produces a lot more ash than wood – far too much to get rid of in an average-sized garden. In addition, a lot of coal, especially 'smokeless' varieties, has other additives in it, which will not do your soil any good if you dig them into the ground.

Cooked Food Scraps, Meat and Fish

Cooked leftovers from your meals, meat, fish, bones, dairy and large quantities of cooking oil should not go into a regular compost heap. You will find out more about processing these in the chapter Compost Bins & Composting Systems (see pages 98–133). In a compost heap they can attract vermin such as rats. Too much cooking oil will clump things together, which will not allow enough oxygen to get into the heap.

Glossy Paper

In the section about what you can compost, there were many types of paper mentioned. There are, however, a few you need to look out for that should not be composted. These include glossy paper such as leaflets sent via junk mail, catalogues, magazines and glossy, foil or holographic wrapping paper. These can contain toxic inks and take a long time to decompose.

Sanitary Protection

Compostable sanitary pads and tampons require the correct levels of heat and moisture to decompose that you probably won't achieve when you begin composting at home. You would also need a specially enclosed vessel so that vermin are not attracted to the pile and you would have to shred everything, removing any adhesives beforehand. For these reasons it is not advisable to compost sanitary protection at home. If you're concerned about the environmental effects of disposable sanitary protection, there are reusable options such as menstrual cups and washable pads.

Synthetics, Metals

Man-made items such as plastics, synthetics, foam, metal, foil or glass should not be put into your compost heap. Most will still be there in a few hundred years' time and they don't add anything of value to your compost.

Recap

You cannot compost:

- Biodegradable nappies
- Cat and dog faeces
- Coal ash
- Cooked food, meat and fish
- Glossy paper
- Sanitary protection
- Synthetics, metals

The Maybe Section

In this section you'll find items that some gardeners say are okay for a compost bin and others say are not. For a beginner, it's probably best to steer clear of these, but once you get the hang of things, you can start to experiment. But if you're not sure, leave it out – there are plenty of safe things to choose from.

Branches, Sticks, Hedge Clippings, Prunings

Depending on size, these can be a useful addition to your compost heap. You'll probably need to treat them first though as large pieces of material will take years to rot down. Twigs can be broken up into short pieces and added occasionally. This is ideal if you have one or two trees in your garden that leave you with a few fallen twigs and a small amount of prunings each year.

Choppity Chop

If you have large sticks, tough hedge clippings and branches to get rid of, you'll need to shred them before you put them on your compost pile. You could borrow or hire a garden shredder for an afternoon to do this, or many local councils have a facility to shred large woody branches, so you could take them there. If you have a large garden, consider leaving a pile of branches and sticks to encourage wildlife. Or you could rot down the tough stuff separately and use it as mulch.

Weeds and Diseased Plants

Whether to add weeds and diseased plants to a compost heap can cause a lot of confusion among people new to composting. Try baking weeds in the sun until they are dry and crispy before adding them to your compost pile. This will kill off any seeds that might cause havoc when you dig the finished compost into your soil. Alternatively, try mixing perennial weeds with grass clippings and 'suffocating' them in a plastic sack until the weeds are no longer recognizable before adding them.

Checklist

- Write down all the things on this list that you **use regularly** at home so that you can see instantly what can and cannot be added to your compost pile.

- Instead of adding cardboard **egg boxes** to your compost pile, why not see if a local farm shop can reuse them?

- If you have a lot of **untreated sawdust** you could offer it to people for animal bedding.

- Don't add too much **paper** to your compost bin. The most ecologically sound thing to do with paper is recycle it.

- When you have your **hair cut** in the spring, do the birds a favour and give them some of your hair for nesting, rather than put it all in the compost bin.

- Even **biodegradable nappies** (diapers) cannot be composted or recycled, why not try cloth nappies (diapers) instead?

- Don't add too many **textiles** to your compost heap; it's better to donate your unwanted items to a charity shop or textiles bank for reuse.

How to Compost?

Composting Basics

By now, you'll know what compost is, good reasons for producing your own compost at home and what to put in the heap. Now you're going to learn how to do it! You might remember seeing the words carbon and nitrogen in the previous chapter. In this chapter you'll learn what they mean and what you need to know about them. Don't worry, this isn't a science book – it's a composting book, so we'll keep things simple and easy to understand.

The Basic Recipe

In order to enjoy good compost, the basic ingredients you need are:

- ✓ Air
- ✓ Warmth
- ✓ Raw ingredients
- ✓ Water

Add patience, a suitable space and a willingness to learn and you've got all you need to provide your soil with nutrient-rich home-made compost. Surveys show that the main reason people don't compost is because they think the process is complicated, time-consuming or specialist equipment is required. This book aims to demystify things and put your mind at ease.

Getting the Ingredients Right

Some people make composting sound so easy! You just throw your stuff in a pile, leave it for a few months and return to find perfect, sweet-smelling compost that feeds your soil and plants. If you've tried that method yourself, you might have faced disappointment. Although home composting *is* easy and doesn't need to be over complicated, time-consuming or require specialist equipment, there are a few key things you need to know. For any good recipe, you need the right ingredients and the right method. It's exactly the same for your compost heap.

Carbon:Nitrogen Mix

Decomposition of organic matter relies on the presence of carbon and nitrogen, which were mentioned briefly in the previous chapter. Now we're going to talk about the carbon:nitrogen ratio or C:N for short. Each type of material you add to the compost heap has a different C:N. If a material has 20 times as much carbon as nitrogen it is said to have a C:N ratio of 20.

Why Is This Ratio Important?

The organisms that decompose organic matter use nitrogen for building themselves up and carbon for energy. It's a bit like us – we need protein to build muscles and for repair and carbohydrates for energy. Just as you feed yourself a good balance of protein and carbohydrates, you need to feed your compost heap a good balance of ingredients too! If you predominantly eat bread, rice and pasta with no protein, your diet won't be very balanced. You might become ill or depleted in certain vital elements of your diet. Think of your compost heap in a similar way.

But What Does This Mean?

In the previous chapter, you would have seen references to grass clippings being high in nitrogen and sawdust being high in carbon. If we take a look at the C:N ratio, we can see that

 Grass clippings are around 19

Sawdust can be up to 500.

Likewise,

 Vegetable peelings are about 19

 Paper has between 200 and 500

You don't need to remember any of these figures and you will no doubt find that different sources give differing figures. What is important is that you begin to get a feel for a pattern...

 The **wetter items** – in this instance grass clippings and vegetable peelings – have a lower carbon:nitrogen ratio. They are higher in nitrogen.

 The **drier items** – in this instance sawdust and paper – have a higher carbon:nitrogen ratio. They are higher in carbon.

Getting the Mix Right

If the compost mix is too low in nitrogen, it will not heat up. If the nitrogen content is too high, the compost may become so hot that it kills the microorganisms. Too much nitrogen can also result in bad-smelling slime. Gardeners talk about trying to achieve a C:N mix of about 30 for best results. Layering your compost heap with different materials can help you achieve this and the end result will have a C:N of around 10. But don't get too hung up on the figures. Just remember that in general the wetter stuff is high in nitrogen and the drier stuff is higher in carbon.

Recap

 Basic ingredients for good compost are **air, organic matter, warmth** and **water**.

Decomposition of organic matter relies on a **good balance** of carbon and nitrogen.

Microorganisms use nitrogen like we use protein and carbon like we use carbohydrate.

 Each item we compost has a different **carbon:nitrogen ratio** (C:N).

 Wetter items have a lower C:N.

 Drier items have a higher C:N.

 If the compost mix is **too low** in nitrogen, it will not heat up.

 If the compost mix is **too high** in nitrogen, the compost may become too hot and kill the microorganisms.

Greens and Browns

If carbon and nitrogen sounds a bit complex, then this section is for you. Instead of nitrogen and carbon, we're going to think in terms of 'green' and 'brown' or 'wet' and 'dry'. You may remember seeing greens and browns mentioned in the previous chapter about what can and cannot go into the compost heap.

The Green to Brown Ratio

Novices to the composting world frequently make the mistake of dumping a load of grass clippings and vegetable peelings on the pile, hoping to see perfect compost in a few months. What actually happens is that they see green slime and this has understandably put many people off compost-making for life!

Greens

Greens are quick to rot and provide important nitrogen and moisture. Greens are the ingredients with a low C:N like grass clippings and vegetable peelings. They are generally new and fresh items rather than old, rotted materials. Young weeds, young plant material and freshly mown grass clippings are all greens.

Too Many Greens are Not Good!

If you have too many of these wet greens in your compost bin, they will quickly turn to slime and begin to smell. It's understandable why so many people experience this, as grass clippings and vegetable peelings are often the most readily available raw ingredients to householders. Many people put them into the heap hoping for healthy compost in a few months. What they end up with, sometimes within a few days, is rotting, slimy green stuff

that smells really bad! Too much nitrogen in the compost heap results in the formation of ammonia – and we know how bad that smells! In addition, this rapid decomposition uses up oxygen, which means that your compost-friendly aerobic microorganisms are replaced by anaerobic ones.

Browns

Browns are slower to rot, provide carbon and let air pockets develop in the compost mix. Browns are ingredients with a high C:N like sawdust. On their own, browns are very slow to decay. You'll know this if you have ever left something like a pile of twigs in the corner of your garden – it can be years before they start to decompose. All but the smallest browns need to be torn up or shredded before adding to the compost pile. If you add too many browns, you will need to add extra greens or water the compost to keep it moist and active. Browns add valuable fibre to your compost heap, which gives a good texture to the end product.

Too Many Browns are Not Good!

If you have too many dry browns in your compost bin, they will sit there for a long time until they eventually decompose. You'll not get compost; you'll just get a pile of browns for ages! As mentioned in the introduction, nature is an expert decomposer, but can take a long time. Shredding things and adding water and greens to the mix will ensure a good chance of success with composting and help balance the amount of browns in the pile.

Recap

 Greens are quick to rot and provide **nitrogen and moisture**. They have a low C:N.

 Too many greens introduce too much nitrogen, which can lead to smelly, rotting slime.

 Browns are slower to rot, provide **carbon** and let **air pockets** develop in the compost mix. They have a high C:N.

 Too many browns will not decompose quickly enough.

 Browns need **shredding** before adding to the compost to expose surface area.

Patterns

Hopefully, you are now seeing a pattern between carbon and nitrogen, browns and greens. Having a grasp of this will help you to create wonderful compost at home.

Brown = high carbon (high C:N) = dry = ingredients like cardboard, sawdust and woody stuff

 Green = high nitrogen (low C:N) = wet = ingredients like grass and kitchen peelings

Put simply, you need a good mix of greens and browns in your compost pile. Using the previous chapter for reference, we can now divide all the useful ingredients into greens (nitrogen-rich), browns (carbon-rich) and those in between (a bit of both). Different references might put the odd thing into different categories, but this is an approximate guide and will help you to get a good C:N in your own compost pile. You can probably guess most of them yourself:

Recap

 Browns are carbon-rich, dry ingredients like cardboard and twigs.

 Greens are nitrogen-rich, wet ingredients like grass clippings and kitchen peelings.

You want a **good mix** of greens and browns by *volume* in your compost bin.

Greens

Chicken manure
Comfrey and nettles
Diluted urine
Fruit and vegetable peelings
Grass cuttings
Seaweed and pondweed
Young plants
Young weeds

Browns

Cardboard
Dried leaves
Paper
Sawdust
Straw
Textiles
Woody branches,
Prunings and trimmings

In-between

Coffee grounds and tea leaves
Dead flowers, pot plants
    and bedding plants
Eggshells
Hair and nail clippings
Old compost from hanging baskets
    and grow bags etc
Soiled vegetarian animal bedding
Vacuum contents and floor sweepings

Hot and Cold Composting

Another term you may have come across is hot (or active) and cold (or passive) composting. Most gardeners do a combination of these methods since it yields good results for the average householder. It is also the method that is emphasized in this book.

Hot Composting

When you hot compost, you gather enough materials to practically fill your container at once. You'll have a good mix of green and brown materials, which might include some old compost, fresh grass clippings, some shredded woody prunings, vegetable peelings, weeds and moist, shredded paper. You mix them together well (you'll have to find a suitable area to do this unless you have two compost areas), then add them to your composting container and cover. As you add the ingredients, you can water them if they need it.

Really Hot!

Using the hot composting technique means that you get an instant blast of heat. Within a couple of days of mixing the ingredients you should start to feel how warm the pile is – you might even see it steaming. This shows you that the compost is working well and that the microbes are busy eating their way through everything. The heat will also help to kill off diseased plants and weed seeds.

Cooling Down

After a week or two, the heap will start to cool down, so you need to turn it. Try to get as much of the outside material towards the centre of the heap as you can; it's a bit like kneading bread! You can check the moisture content of the heap at this point. If it's too dry, add some water or if it is too wet, add some more shredded paper or cardboard. If at all possible, turning the heap should involve getting all the ingredients back out of the container, mixing thoroughly, watering any dry areas and putting it all back in again before covering. It's labour intensive, but worth it for quick composting.

Turn Again

Turning the heap like this will generate some extra heat to get the decomposition process more active again. You can repeat the turning and mixing of ingredients again if you wish, but you will not get the initial burst of heat you had when you originally put the materials together. During the first two weeks when things were really hot, the microorganisms were eating through the soft greens. Now the tougher stuff, the browns, need to be eaten, and this happens at cooler temperatures and is carried out by different creatures in the compost. As the compost cools, leave it alone to allow the decomposition process to finish. Once the compost has cooled down, continuing to turn it will not be an advantage.

Pros

 You can be using your compost in as little as **12 weeks**.
 Diseased plants and weed seeds will be killed.

Cons

 Needs care and attention and a large amount of **raw ingredients**.
 Takes more **time and energy**, so not for the time poor or those who are unable to turn all the materials at once.

Cold Composting

Cold composting is a more passive form of composting. To do this you put an initial couple of layers of ingredients into your compost bin. At least 30 cms (12 in) is recommended for the first layer. Remember to mix greens and browns to get a good carbon:nitrogen ratio. Continue adding ingredients as and when you have them, such as kitchen peelings, grass clippings, shredded paper, shredded hedge prunings and torn toilet roll inners. The compost container will gradually fill up, but if you don't add much material, it will rot down as quickly as you can fill it; especially during the summer months.

Slowly Does It

With cold composting, you stop adding ingredients either after 6 months or when the compost bin is full — whichever comes first. Then you leave everything for up to a year. At the end of this time, you should find some rich compost at the bottom of the pile. Dig this out and use it on your garden. The rest of the ingredients can be mixed up, ready to start your next batch of compost. You can check the moisture levels and adjust them if necessary; either by the addition of some water or of something dry, such as a little sawdust. After that, leave everything to mature and continue with the composting process again.

Pros

 Requires **little effort**, so great for a time-constrained gardener.

 Ideal for households that produce **little waste**.

 Good for those with **physical limitations** as mixing and turning is minimal.

Cons

 Can take a **long time** to produce compost.

 Best not to add **diseased or tenacious weeds** as they might survive the process.

A Bit of Both

Most people will do a mixture of the two methods. The average householder does not produce an entire compost heap's worth of ingredients at once, so it's simpler to add things to the pile as you create them. By turning the compost heap every couple of weeks or so you'll warm things up, which will increase the rate of decomposition. The theory goes that the more frequently you turn the heap, the quicker your compost will be ready.

Recap

 Hot composting is known as active composting.

 Hot composting involves **filling a bin** with materials in one go.

 Hot composting generally results in **quicker compost**.

 With hot composting you need to **turn the ingredients** at least once.

 Cold composting is known as passive composting.

 Cold composting involves adding materials **as and when**.

 Cold composting is a **slower** composting process.

 Cold composting is **less physical work** than hot composting.

This book focuses on a **mix** of both hot and cold composting – adding things as you find them and turning occasionally, which is perfect for most householders.

How to Layer Your Compost Pile

Now you know all about the carbon and nitrogen ratio, or greens and browns, you're ready to start your compost heap. Making good compost is a bit like making a good sandwich. You're going to layer up the ingredients to create something that tastes good for all the microbes in your compost heap! If you make a sandwich with just bread, it's not a sandwich and if you make a sandwich with just cheese, it's not a sandwich. Think of your compost heap like this – if you add all greens or all browns you won't have the right ingredients.

Basic Layering 'Recipe'

There are various 'recipes', but nothing is set in stone and as long as you are aware of the browns and greens ratio you won't go far wrong. Don't worry too much at this point if things are starting to seem a bit complex and don't get hung up on the carbon and nitrogen figures either. Once you get out there and start adding things to the heap, everything will make sense.

Let's Begin

Let's not overcomplicate things here. You don't have to create something pretty and perfect; you just need to create something that works! So what if your layers aren't equal? Layering is simply a technique to help you get used to balancing the greens and browns of your compost heap. When you plant a seed or plant in a pot, what is the first thing you do? Ensure the pot has drainage holes and then add a layer of stones or broken crocks so that the roots don't become waterlogged. That is exactly what you are going to do with your compost heap.

First Steps

To ensure the bottom of the compost heap does not get slimy, put in a layer of something brown, such as twigs, or shredded woody prunings. Make it a good layer, a few inches or so, as this will help to increase the flow of air around the compost pile. This is better than using cardboard or paper because these materials will eventually soak up the water and stay wet. Now you can begin layering – equal layers of green stuff and brown stuff. You don't add equal quantities by weight; you do it by *volume*, which is much easier and doesn't rely on a set of scales!

Easy Layering

If all that sounds a bit too time-consuming or off-putting then you can layer more simply. The reality in most households is that you produce far more greens than browns. Fruit and vegetable peelings and mown grass are the most common offerings. If you keep a container in your kitchen for peelings, then simply match this with a container of shredded paper or straw. Keep hold of old newspapers or junk mail for this purpose. Once you've got a grass box full of grass clippings then match it with a grass box full of torn up cardboard and throw it all into your compost heap! You'll get a feel for working with volumes in this way. A container full of vegetable peelings or grass clippings weighs much more than a container full of dry twigs. Remember, it's *volume* that matters, not weight.

More Structured

Some people prefer a step-by-step 'recipe'. If you do, then this is for you!

 Layer 1: 6–12 cm (3–5 in) of twigs or woody material for good drainage.

 Layer 2: 6–12 cm (3–5 in) of old compost or good quality garden soil to introduce microorganisms.

 Layer 3: 6–12 cm (3–5 in) of kitchen waste to attract worms and bacteria.

Layer 4: 6–12 cm (3–5 in) of moistened and shredded cardboard or paper to get the balance of greens and browns right.

 Layer 5: 6–12 cm (3–5 in) of grass clippings; another green layer.

 Layer 6: 6–12 cm (3–5 in) of shredded woody prunings; another brown layer and so on...

You'll notice that for best results, organic waste should be put in the bin in layers of 6–12 cm (3–5 in) deep. Once you've put in the initial twigs, old compost and kitchen waste layers, you then continue with whatever greens and browns you have; adding them as and when. Keep things warm and moist and nature should take care of the rest.

Simple Rules

The basic rule is that if your compost starts to get wet and sloppy, you need to add more browns such as scrunched-up newspaper or shredded cardboard. If it gets too dry, you need to add more of the wetter greens, such as grass cuttings or vegetable peelings or even water the heap a little. It's like baking bread in the great outdoors – you add a little more flour or water to get the right dough.

Recap

 Layering ensures a good mix of greens and browns.

 Layering will help you get used to the **right balance** of ingredients, but is not essential.

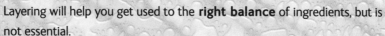 Put a layer of woody **twigs** in the bottom of your heap for good **drainage**.

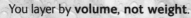 You layer by **volume, not weight**.

 You can layer by simply adding the same volume of **greens to browns** whenever you add something new to the pile.

 If your compost gets **too wet** or smells, add more browns.

 If your compost gets **too dry** and doesn't decompose, water the pile or add more greens.

Practical Composting

The other potential problem the householder can face is lack of availability of a good mix of raw ingredients. During the summer, for example, there might be a glut of grass clippings, young plants and fruit peelings – the greens. During the autumn many of us have a plethora of dead leaves and woody prunings – the browns. Browns are pretty easy to store. They are dry and won't decompose readily. You can add some torn up cardboard and scrunched newspaper and store everything until needed. Then when you add a pile of grass clippings, you have your browns on hand to create the perfect recipe.

Where to Site Your Compost Area

Regardless of whether you use an open heap, a bin or any of the other choices laid out in later chapters, you need to think about where your compost area will be situated. It needs to be practical for you, otherwise you might not bother. You don't want to have to walk half a mile to feed it with your kitchen peelings. Neither do you want it too far from the place you will use your finished compost.

Let the Party Begin

Remember that the microorganisms and worms will usually move in to your new heap of their own accord, but you'll make it much easier for them if you put your compost area on bare soil. If you have clay soil, loosen the soil a little first with a fork to improve drainage and give the worms and bacteria a head start with finding your bin!

A Hard Surface

If you can only place your bin on concrete or similar, then you might want to stuff newspapers or some other absorbent material around the base to prevent the liquid run-off chasing you every time you feed the bin! This will help prevent staining the surface of your patio or decking. You may also need to add some worms yourself. The easiest way to do this is to 'borrow' a handful of worms from someone with a well-established compost heap. Alternatively, you can buy them from some garden centres and specialist online stores.

Run-off

Compost piles tend to leak from the base of the heap. This is the result of the breakdown of organic matter in your bin. This doesn't matter if it's situated on well-drained soil, but you might not be so happy if this happens on your clean patio or decking. Ideally, you would capture this 'liquid gold' and use it as a fertilizer, as it is rich in minerals and nutrients, which some plants love. Unfortunately most people simply let it run into the ground.

Capturing Run-off

If you buy plant fertilizer every year, why not start gathering your own liquid feed – a great by-product of your home composting. It's a gift that will be well received by any

Have You Thought Of?

An earthworm can eat up to half its own body weight in one day!

gardening friends too. It is simplest to do this if you are using some kind of specially bought compost bin, as it's virtually impossible to gather from beneath an open heap. You'll need to elevate the bin, perhaps on some old house bricks or wooden blocks and put a tray underneath to catch the liquid. Dilute this liquid with three parts water to use on plants.

Temperature Control

Remember that your compost heap will work more efficiently the hotter it gets, so choose a sunny and sheltered spot. This is particularly important if you choose to have an open heap. It will need protecting from the wind and rain. Not only can rain make the ingredients too wet, but they cool the heap down as well. This is easily rectified with an old piece of carpet, large piece of polythene or tarpaulin used as a cover.

Recap

 Store browns for easy addition to your compost pile.

 Put your compost bin **somewhere handy** – close enough to add kitchen and household waste and near to your garden beds.

 Site your compost bin on **bare soil** if possible to attract worms and friendly bacteria.

 Choose a **sunny, well-sheltered spot** for your compost bin.

Keep the **rain** out of your compost bin with a cover.

Try and capture the liquid **run-off** from your compost pile; it's nutrient-rich plant food.

How to Influence Your Compost Pile

Sometimes your compost heap will have a few problems. In this section you will find techniques for influencing your compost pile. These include aeration, temperature, moisture, organisms, shredding and additives and activators. A careful balance of these can help you to get the most out of your compost heap. In a later chapter, you will find out about specific composting problems and how to deal with them.

Aeration

Whenever you add something new to the compost heap, bear in mind that the microorganisms need air to survive and be active. For example, if you put too many grass clippings or vegetable peelings on your heap, the ingredients will compress down and stop air getting in. Air is vital to the compost heap since decomposition will slow down and may eventually stop if oxygen is not replenished. Trap air in the compost heap as you build it up using carbon-rich materials such as cardboard and twigs. When you add browns such as paper or cardboard, don't just throw flat sheets in; you'll need to shred, tear or scrunch them up so that they can break down easily.

Tip

Construct the heap or bin on a stand to increase airflow

Turning the Pile

Turning the compost pile is the most common way of introducing oxygen into the heap. Air is as vital to your compost heap as it is to you. Aerobic microorganisms need oxygen to survive, so don't suffocate the heap by throwing too many wet greens in there at once.

As the temperature of the ingredients drops, turning them helps raise the temperature again, because of the replenished oxygen supply. Mixing things up means that the organic materials not yet decomposed have a chance of being composted. Unfortunately, turning the heap is one of the reasons why many people do not bother with composting; it all seems like too much effort. Fortunately, there are ways to make this easier, which you will find out about in later chapters.

Easier Ways to Turn

Purist gardeners will take the contents out of their hot heap, mix them about and return them to the compost bin as outlined in the section about hot composting. This is great and works really well, but if you're physically unable to do this or don't have time, don't worry – there are plenty of other ways to make sure your heap is getting enough air. Choose one of the following methods:

 Mix things as best you can with a **garden fork**.

 Use a specially designed compost **aerator**.

 Use a **broom handle** to poke holes throughout the mix.

 Make sure you add **scrunched up** paper, a handful of twigs or torn up cardboard egg boxes every time you add greens to create pockets of air.

Recap

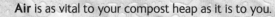

- **Air** is as vital to your compost heap as it is to you.
- **Adding browns** when you add greens creates better aeration.
- **Turning the** pile adds oxygen.
- **Shred**, **tear or cut** woody browns to create air pockets.
- **Mixing** things well with a garden fork or a compost aerator introduces oxygen.
- **Scrunch up** newspaper and shred cardboard before adding – never add flat sheets.

Temperature

The organisms in your compost heap need warmth to stay active. As the organic matter decomposes it produces heat, so the centre of your compost heap will nearly always be warm. During the winter, you can cover the heap with old carpet or insulate the sides with straw to keep things snug throughout the colder months. Decomposition will slow down during the winter, but not stop altogether unless your climate is really cold. You may well find that your compost heap is full at some point, but check it again a few weeks later and it is likely that there will be room for new ingredients where raw materials have decomposed. The temperature of the compost pile is a good indication of how fast the decomposition process is taking place.

Influencing Temperature

Heat is a natural by-product of the breakdown of organic material, but other factors also affect the warmth of your compost heap. A small pile will not get as warm as a large pile, so if you allow your compost to break down without adding new material it will get colder. The initial size of the pile or bin is something to take into consideration when setting up your compost area. Recommendations for the minimum size are around 1 m (3 ft) wide, 1 m (3 ft) deep and 1 m (3 ft) high; more about that later. As well as the outdoor temperature affecting the compost temperature, the moisture content and airflow will have an influence too.

An Outdoor Fire

A compost heap is a bit like an open fire. For a fire to continue burning it needs the triangle of fuel, heat and air; similarly, your compost heap requires raw ingredients (fuel), heat and air, as well as the

Tip
Feed your compost big meals!

critters that eat through the raw materials. It is the composting process that produces heat, so heating your pile it is not simply a case of adding more heat from the outside – this on its own won't work. An easy way to ensure a warm pile is to think about where you will site it. A sunny spot, away from high winds and protected from rainfall, is ideal. You can also increase the heat of your compost by adding quite a lot of mixed materials at once, say two or three days' worth of stuff, rather than drip-feeding your compost pile daily.

Reasons Why Your Compost Heap Might Not Get Hot Enough

If the pile does not heat up, common reasons include:

 The heap is **too wet**, limiting the oxygen that bacteria require.
 The heap is **too dry** for the bacteria to survive and reproduce.
 There is **insufficient protein** (nitrogen-rich material).
 The heap is **too large** and starved of oxygen on the inside.
 The heap is **too small** and losing internal heat.

The necessary material should be added, or the pile should be turned to aerate it and bring the outer layers inside and vice versa. You should add water at this time if the ingredients are not damp enough.

Recap

Organisms in your compost heap need warmth to stay active.

Keep your compost heap warm by **covering** it with an old carpet.

You can **insulate** your compost in the winter with straw.

An **active** compost heap will stay warm even during the winter, except in the most extreme of climates.

A **small** compost heap cannot get as warm as a large one.

Adding a lot of **materials**, rather than a few at a time, can raise the heat of your compost.

Moisture

Just like you, the microorganisms, insects and worms in your compost heap need water to survive. It's not just a case of dumping a load of water on the pile though. Too much water will result in a heap of smelly slime, and that is what we are trying to avoid at all costs! Water is present in nitrogen-rich materials such as grass cuttings and vegetable peelings. During a hot, dry summer you can add a little water to the heap if it gets too dry.

Not Too Wet, Not Too Dry

The right moisture levels in your compost bin are something you will soon get used to. The ingredients should be like a well-wrung sponge – just damp, so that if you squeeze hard a couple of drops of water drip out. Too little moisture inhibits bacterial activity, as is the case with too many browns. Too much moisture results in slow decomposition and produces a slimy mess. Avoid too much water by keeping the compost covered so that the rain doesn't get in there.

Add Greens

To introduce moisture to your pile without watering it, add some greens, such as vegetable peelings or grass clippings, when you add drier browns. However, be careful not to add too many greens at once otherwise the heap might get too wet.

Recap

- **Microorganisms**, insects and worms in your compost heap need water to survive.
- **Too much water** will result in slime – take it easy with the greens!
- The ingredients should be like a **well-wrung sponge**.
- Avoid too much water by protecting your compost heap from the **rain**.
- In a **hot climate**, check your heap is not becoming too dry through evaporation.

Activators

If you are starting a compost heap from scratch, it may need a helping hand. This is where activators come in. Activators literally activate the heap – they get things going. They are also useful if the composting process slows down or it looks like things have stopped working. Some garden centres sell specially designed activator products available as liquid or granules. These are sold under various names, but all have the aim of helping you make stress-free compost. However, all you really need is a little know-how and you'll probably find you have access to some free activators already! Great activators include:

Chicken manure
 Comfrey
Diluted urine
 Nettles
A spade full of soil or compost

Tip

Paper and cardboard are great brown ingredients because they soak up water, keeping things moist.

Ways to Activate Your Compost Heap

An important first step for good activation is the placement of your compost heap. You need to allow bacteria, insects and worms access to your heap. Situating your pile on good soil is the key. Add a few spades of soil or quality compost to the compost heap when you set it up and you'll incorporate some beneficial microorganisms, which will ensure a high level of activity in your compost.

Chicken Manure

If you keep chickens then you're ahead of the game. If not, perhaps a neighbour or friend can help you out by giving you a bag of chicken manure in return for some compost later in the year. Many people keep pigeons, so it should not be difficult to get hold of pigeon droppings, whether you live in the town or the country. Our pigeon and chicken friends provide us with a great compost activator, so ask around or look for adverts in your local paper. Many people are happy to give manure away to gardeners. Alternatively try your local www.freecycle.org group.

Comfrey

Comfrey should be in everyone's garden somewhere! It grows like a weed and can grow tall and wide, so contain it if this will be a problem. It's virtually impossible to kill, so bear this in mind when you plant it – it's a plant for life! Comfrey enriches a compost heap and encourages it to heat up. You can add some leaves to your compost pile or make comfrey tea (see below).

Using Comfrey Leaves

Once you have added the first layers to your compost heap, checking the water content and brown to green ratio is right, spread 2½–5 cm (1–2 in) fresh comfrey leaves over the surface of your heap. Sprinkle with water and add a fine layer of soil.

Comfrey Tea

Comfrey tea is simple to make. Fill a bucket or tub with comfrey leaves, cover with water, pop a lid on and leave for a month. The result will smell like something unmentionable, but don't let that put you off! The strained liquid can be added to your compost heap or used as a tomato fertilizer. You can also line a trench with wilted comfrey leaves before planting potatoes. This increases their yield and improves the flavour. Throw any remaining wet leaves into the compost pile.

Nettles

Most of us view nettles as a nuisance weed, but they are extremely valuable to the gardener. Using nettles as an activator for your compost heap is a simple case of gathering the leaves and adding them. Wear gloves to protect your hands from being stung. Nettles provide a nitrogen-rich addition to your compost heap that will help to get things going.

Urine

There's no excuse not to add this one as we all have access to copious amounts of it! Urine can be diluted with water up to 20 times before adding, so wee in a bottle and add water. Then add this diluted mix to the compost heap. This will save you money on nitrogen-rich compost activators bought from the garden centre. Nobody needs to know what you are doing; you can keep things discreet. And think of the water you will save on flushing the toilet!

Don't Forget Your Greens

Greens act as activators. The microorganisms that are going to eat their way through your raw materials need these to start work so make sure you are adding things like grass clippings, young weeds, vegetable peelings and plant materials. Remember not to get the compost pile too wet when adding greens. If necessary, introduce some carbon-rich, dry browns at the same time such as shredded paper or cardboard.

Shredding, Tearing and Cutting

As mentioned previously, your compost heap needs air in order for decomposition to take place. You can achieve this by turning the pile, but the easiest way to do it is to ensure a good mix of greens and browns. Browns, by their physical nature, help to bring air into the compost heap. They are more bulky and create air pockets. Twigs, for example, provide a rough structure for air to flow freely through. If the woody pieces are too large, however, such as branches or some hedge prunings, then they can take far too long to decompose.

Size Matters!

By shredding large branches, tearing cardboard and scrunching up newspaper, you can help your compost heap no end. It makes large materials like branches less bulky, speeding up their decomposition, and scrunching newspaper allows oxygen to flow through to the rest of the ingredients. You should never put flat sheets of newspaper or cardboard into a compost heap. All that will happen is that they will soak up moisture and provide a kind of barrier to the airflow around the compost, rather than facilitating it. Shred office paper before use too.

Organisms

It's rare that you need to add organisms to your compost heap. It's the most magical part of composting – these helpful critters just seem to appear from nowhere and start working! Let's face it, if you're providing food, warmth and favourable conditions, they'd be crazy not to move in and live there – it's free bed and board. If they don't move in, which can happen if the compost bin is not situated on bare soil, then you can introduce them with a spade full of old compost or garden soil.

Bought activators

You can buy other activators such as herbal preparations and composting microbes from garden centres. However, if your compost heap is healthy then you don't need to interfere or add things. Just be patient and allow the natural processes to work. Often we expect results too quickly – nature needs time to do her job. Remember we are co-operating, not competing, so sit out in the garden, enjoy your surroundings and be patient. The best things in life are worth waiting for!

Recap

 Natural and free **activators** include poultry manure, comfrey, nettles, urine and a spade full of compost.

 Site your compost heap on **bare soil** to encourage worms, bacteria and insects.

 A **spade full of soil** or compost will introduce a beneficial ecosystem into your compost.

 Learn to love your weeds! **Nettles** are great activators.

 Find room for **comfrey** if you can – it's a gardener's friend.

 Urine is a good activator; dilute and add to your compost heap.

 A **good mix** of green and shredded browns should mean that your compost works well and will activate itself.

Additives

Some gardeners swear by using additives in their compost heap. These add a variety of trace minerals and elements or help alter the pH of your compost heap. Other gardeners do not feel they are necessary in a healthy garden; however, it can be useful to know about some of them.

Agricultural Lime

Sometimes, the compost bin can become too acidic and the pH drops. This is often the case if too many vegetable peelings are added or if it is not aerated properly. A light dusting of agricultural lime can help, sprinkled onto the kitchen peelings. If lack of air is the problem, then try other methods first such as turning the heap or adding more browns.

pH

Don't get too worried about the pH of your compost. Compost piles become acidic in the initial stages anyway and as the process continues, the pH rises again. Finished compost usually has a pH of between 6 and 8. Bear in mind that compost microorganisms operate best under neutral to acidic conditions, so don't add too much lime and make your compost heap over-alkaline!

Rock Flour

Some gardeners use rock flour to restore trace minerals to their soil. You can add rock flour to your compost, which will then be dug into the earth to replace these minerals. There is a lot of information available about the demineralization of our soils and general soil depletion caused by intensive farming and forestry that you might like to read up on. If you feel that your soil is depleted, then rock flour may be a useful addition to your compost heap. In addition, you can employ methods such as rotation of crops and green manuring to help with soil depletion in your garden.

Seaweed Meal

Seaweed meal provides trace elements and can be used as a compost activator. If you don't have access to fresh seaweed, then buying it dry from a garden centre or online store can provide a valuable addition to your compost heap and will enrich your soil. Seaweed is rich in calcium, which is an important component of your compost.

Recap

- ☑ There are a variety of compost **additives** readily available.
- ☑ **Agricultural lime** can reduce acidity.
- ☑ **Rock flour** contains important trace minerals.
- ☑ **Seaweed meal** is a good activator and contains elements such as calcium.

When Is My Compost Ready?

This is the moment you've been waiting for. You've been tending to your compost heap, lovingly feeding it with all your waste, and now you want to use it on your garden. But how do you know when it's ready? How do you know when that wonderful moment has arrived? Is it really going to look like the stuff you have been buying in bags? And what if it doesn't?

Appearance of Finished Compost

Finished compost bears no resemblance to the original ingredients. It will be dark brown or black, pretty dry and rich looking. It looks like the best quality topsoil you could ever hope for and will have shrunk considerably – up to a half of its original volume. If you are hot composting, the heap will no longer be producing any heat.

Texture of Finished Compost

Good compost is fine and crumbly, but it can vary in texture according to the original ingredients. You'll learn about this first hand as you create more batches of compost. Some compost is quite lumpy, you might find the odd small stick or bits of eggshell in it. Sometimes it is stringy, containing bits of straw or cellulose. It can even be a bit sticky. You don't need to worry about any of this, if the smell is right, then it is okay. If you prefer, you can sieve the compost before using it and throw any big pieces back into the compost pile for the next batch. It's beneficial to use some of your old compost to start a new pile anyway, because it contains beneficial microorganisms.

Smell of Finished Compost

Earthy smelling, sweet and rich; good compost has the kind of smell that makes you want to inhale deeply as it has such a feel-good scent. You just want to dig your hands in and keep on breathing it in! It smells like the most beautiful damp woodland, or soil after a bout of rain in the summer.

If Your Compost Is Not Ready

If, despite the compost looking and smelling right, you are still unsure then here is an idea. The compost you buy in bags has been sealed in plastic for months and it never smells, so why not try the following at home:

Take a **handful of compost** from the centre of your pile.

Moisten it a little and seal it in a **plastic bag**.

Keep this bag at **room temperature** for a week, then open the bag and take a sniff.

If it **smells like soil**, it's ready; if it smells a bit rotten then it's not.

Don't Worry!

If your compost is not ready then don't worry. Although you might be tempted to use your compost sooner than it is finished, it is better to wait. Compost that is still processing can burn tender plants if you use it around them, so don't rush things. Patience is the key! If this happens to you, then you will need to 'cure' the pile. Simply leave it alone and let nature do its work. This process literally allows the compost to finish off, just like wine and cheese are left to mature.

The Curing Process

There's nothing amazing about the curing process; it basically means that you leave well alone! Mix everything up again, make sure the moisture levels are okay – add more water if necessary, pile it back into the compost bin and wait. The curing process can take anything from a month to a year.

How to Speed Up the Composting Process

The general rule with composting is similar to most things in life – the more work you put in, the quicker the results. Some gardeners pride themselves on taking just a few weeks to create compost. Using a more passive process might take a year or more. Neither one is better than the other; it all depends on your lifestyle and any time, space or energy constraints you might have. The main thing is that you have a go and start composting. All the while you are experiencing making your own compost you are learning something new and doing your bit for the environment.

When Two Is Better Than One

Compost does take a while to make, so if you have the room it is better to have two compost heaps: one which is rotting down, or 'cooking', and another which you are adding fresh ingredients to. Some gardeners have three compost heaps – one which is 'cooking', one which is being added to and a third which is being used. This is not to say that you cannot manage with one pile, but if you do have the space then you'll be able to make more compost and you won't have to wait so long to use it because there will always be a pile that is ready.

Have You Thought Of?

How much your landfill waste will be reduced once you are composting?

Is Frequent Turning Better?

Turning the heap is a good way to speed things up. If you remember, turning the heap adds oxygen, which heats things up and gets all those lovely organisms hungry and active. You can turn your compost weekly to fortnightly if you wish. Some gardeners say that the more you turn the ingredients, the quicker things happen; some don't. As with everything in life, experiment, experience things and find out what works best for you!

Recap

- ✔ **Finished compost** bears no resemblance to the original ingredients.
- ✔ Finished compost has a **pleasant, earthy smell** and is crumbly.
- ✔ Do the **plastic bag trick** if you are not sure whether your compost is ready or not.
- ✔ Don't use your compost **too early**; you could do irreparable damage to plants.
- ✔ **Be patient**! Your compost might need some curing time.
- ✔ If you have room, set up **two or even three compost bins** to ensure a continual supply.

Checklist

✓ Review the pattern between **greens and browns**, **carbon and nitrogen**, **wet and dry** ingredients so that you have a better understanding of the requirements of your compost heap.

✓ Think of an **average week** in your household – what green and brown items do you come across regularly?

✓ Decide **where to put** your compost bin – choose a sheltered spot, preferably on bare soil.

✓ Find a source of **natural activators**; do you have nettles or comfrey in your garden or a source of poultry manure? If not, your own urine is the answer!

✓ Decide how much **space and time** you can dedicate to composting and start making a plan.

✓ Start stockpiling some **useful browns** such as shredded cardboard, scrunched up newspaper and small twigs.

✓ Do you need to 'borrow' some **worms** or compost from a friend to get things started? If so, organize this.

Compost Bins & Composting Systems

Compost Bins

No matter what size garden you have, how many raw ingredients your household produces or how much time you have for gardening, there will be a compost bin to suit you. Compost areas range from huge open heaps to compact plastic bins, with everything in between!

Deciding Which Type to Get

There are several questions you need to ask yourself before deciding on the best compost bin for your needs:

 What **volume of materials** will you be composting?

 What **space** do you have in your garden for composting?

 Do you need **more than one** compost bin?

 What is your **budget**?

 How much **time and energy** do you have?

Once you have decided on these five factors, you can begin to make a choice about the type of compost bin most suited to your lifestyle. In this chapter you'll learn more about each type.

Moulded Plastic Compost Bins

One of the most popular types of composting bin is an enclosed plastic style. These are usually black or green and often made from recycled plastic. They are mostly made from one moulded piece and have a lid. They are suitable for small or medium gardens and are great for fitting in with a busy lifestyle. You can just feed the bin in small amounts and turn the contents occasionally.

All Sorts of Shapes

The majority of moulded plastic compost bins are cylindrical or cone-shaped and are frequently referred to as 'daleks' due to their construction. Cylindrical composters have no corners, which is advantageous as mixing is easier and there are no areas where organic material can get stuck and dry out or get slimy. Rectangular shaped bins are handy if space is an issue because they can fit right up against walls and fences. Be aware that pushing plastic bins right up against wooden fences can make the fence rot more quickly.

All Sorts of Sizes

Plastic bins range in size from around 220 litres (48 gallons) to about 450 litres (99 gallons) or bigger. A small 200 litre (44 gallon) bin is ideal for a one-person household or those with a small garden. Larger bins are better for a bigger family with a small- to medium-sized garden.

Water Retention

As seen in previous chapters, microorganisms need food, air, water and warmth to thrive. Due to their plastic construction, these types of bin hold moisture well. Don't, however, buy one that has air holes in the sides. They might seem like a good idea, for airflow, but moisture loss will be a problem, potentially resulting in a lack of decomposition. If you are given a bin like this, line it first with corrugated cardboard, which will eventually disintegrate into the mix. It is better to pre-soak browns before adding them to a moulded plastic compost bin rather than watering the bin, as the water tends to run down to the bottom and not reach the contents in the middle of the heap. A few air holes at the bottom of the bin, however, are fine.

Keeping the Heat in

Keeping heat in the compost pile is essential for good decomposition. A cone that is narrower at the top than the bottom helps to reduce heat loss since heat rises. The downside is it can be more difficult to get the finished compost out of the bin if there is no hatch at the bottom. So bear this in mind if you choose a cone-shaped bin.

Retrieving the Compost

Some styles require that you lift the entire bin off the finished compost. Others have a lid that you open in order to dig the compost out. Some have a hatch at the bottom that you lift up to get to the compost. A garden hoe is ideal for reaching your finished contents if you have a hatch, otherwise you will need to fork the contents out into a wheelbarrow. This can be hard work if your only access is through the lid as some plastic bins are quite tall, making this job awkward. In addition, the finished compost is likely to be at the bottom of the bin, not at the top, so if your only access is the lid, then you need to dig out all the rotting stuff first. Check the size of the hatch before purchasing a plastic compost bin; some hatches are so tiny they are virtually useless for removing the finished product.

> **Tip**
>
> Scatter a thin layer of finished compost or rich garden soil over every 15 cm (6 in) or so of new material to maintain good levels of microorganisms.

Getting the Most From a Plastic-moulded Bin

To aerate the contents of a plastic bin, you'll need an aerating tool or garden fork. Plunge the aerating tool or fork into the middle of the pile and lever it around to mix things up and break down any clumps of raw material. As these types of bins hold only a small amount, you'll need to keep adding new ingredients. They aren't much good for hot (active) composting. Their size means that they give less prolonged intense heat, so adding new ingredients and aerating the contents from time to time is the key to success.

Expense

Plastic compost bins are popular because they are inexpensive to buy, they help you reduce landfill waste and provide you with decent compost. Many people report their bin lasting for over ten years with no need for repair or maintenance. However, in a hot, dry climate, it has been reported that plastic compost bins can become brittle after one year.

Pros

- **No assembly** or maintenance required.
- Often made from **recycled materials**.
- **Lightweight**, so can be moved easily.
- Good for **smaller gardens**.
- **Inexpensive**.
- Good **moisture retention** and windproof.

Cons

- Only **produces a small amount** of compost.
- Can be **difficult to get** the finished compost **out**.
- **Lids can be flimsy** if you are adding ingredients daily; lids and hinges can break
- Can be prone to **heat loss**, so aerate from time to time.
- Only **holds a small amount** of materials, so no good for hot composting.
- In a cold climate, single-skinned plastic may **cool down** considerably in the winter.
- In a hot climate, plastic may become **brittle**.

Look out for

Make sure the bin is open at the bottom to allow microorganisms in and nutrient-rich liquid fertilizer out.

Self-assembly Plastic Bins

The second type of compost bin is also made from plastic; often recycled. These are self-assembly types, which come in flat packs. Home assembly is required, but they do not need any specialist tools as most styles simply click together.

All Sorts of Shapes

Most self-assembly bins are square, octagonal or hexagonal, depending on size. Compost bins with straight sides are easier to site in most gardens, as they will fit into a corner. However,

it's best not to push these up against a wooden fence as the fence can deteriorate more quickly. One consideration with straight-sided bins is that you have to ensure a good mix of contents. If you don't, you might end up with raw ingredients stuck in the corners drying out or turning slimy. Hexagonal bins take up a surprising amount of space, so bear this in mind before purchasing.

All Sorts of Sizes

Self-assembly compost bins range from around 200 litres (44 gallons), which is suitable for a small garden, to 800 litres (176 gallons), which is great for a larger garden or family who produce a lot of garden and kitchen waste. Straight-sided bins can be easier to site, especially if you want to put two bins side by side.

Water Retention

Self-assembly compost bins often have slatted sides, meaning there are gaps between each piece. This is designed for good airflow but, as with the moulded bins, can mean that the ingredients dry out too quickly. This is easily rectified; just soak browns such as shredded cardboard and paper before adding them to the bin to add moisture. Another solution is to line the sides of the bin with large sheets of cardboard and to keep the bin in a sheltered area.

Keeping the Heat In

Nearly all types of self-assembly plastic bin come with a robust, hinged lid to help keep the heat in your heap. Choosing a larger bin gives you a better chance of heat retention and occasionally turning your heap with an aerator or fork can help introduce more oxygen, which raises the heat.

Tip

Look for one made from recycled plastic to give your eco-credentials a boost.

Retrieving the Compost

An advantage of this style of bin is easy access to the finished product. Most styles come with a hinged lid and a kind of door that opens halfway down for you to retrieve the finished compost. In addition, some styles come with a good-sized hatch at the bottom. Often these types of bin will open on more than just one side, so there is good all-round access to your rich compost.

Getting the Most from Self-assembly Compost Bins

Some models come with adjustable slats so that you can control the airflow. This can be useful and gives you added control over the conditions inside your compost bin. For beginners, however, this might mean one more confusing thing to think about, so it might be better to use these once you are familiar with the composting process.

Expense

These types of compost bin are reasonably priced and readily available. They cost slightly more than the moulded plastic compost bins but are more attractive to look at.

Pros

 Provide **easy access** to the compost, even with small bins.

 Easy to assemble without tools.

Often made from **recycled materials**.

 Larger bins have **doors on all sides** allowing access to fresh compost from every angle.

Cons

 Many are made with gaps or air holes, which can result in **moisture loss**.

 Not suitable for those who wish to **avoid plastic** on environmental grounds.

Hexagonal bins can look nice but take up a **lot of room**.

Look out for

Try and select a model with adjustable vents so that you can control the airflow.

Flat-pack Wood Slats

Flat-pack wooden-slatted compost bins require simple home assembly. All you need to do is slot together the pre-cut slats to make a square, wooden tower.

All Sorts of Shapes

Most wooden slatted compost bins requiring home assembly are square; this makes them quick to assemble and it easy to find a convenient site. Most are free-standing and do not require you to dig holes for posts. Some models come with a slatted base as an optional extra.

All Sorts of Sizes

These bins come in various sizes, but are often modular so that you can easily create a system of two or three compost areas – one full of finished compost, one 'cooking' and one being added to. If you want to hot compost, the minimum size recommended is 1 m (3 ft) long, by 1 m (3 ft) wide, by 1 m (3 ft) high – to enable a sufficiently high temperature.

Tip

Choose Forest Stewardship Council (FSC) certified timber for extra ecofriendliness..

Water Retention

The slatted design means that water can be lost through air gaps. You'll need to add damp materials, such as pre-soaked cardboard, or line the bin with cardboard sheets to avoid too much moisture loss. A lid helps too. Some companies offer close-boarded varieties – these don't have the air gaps so are better at retaining water. In these bins you can either hot (active) compost or easily aerate with a fork or aerator.

Keeping the Heat In

Wood has good insulating properties. Be aware that lids often come as an optional extra so you will need to add this figure to your budget or be prepared to make your own. Old pieces of carpet, tarpaulin, plastic sheeting or corrugated metal make ideal lids. But if it's good looks you are after, then you'll need to buy the lid as well.

Retrieving the Compost

Retrieving the compost from these bins is easy as you simply remove the slats at the front, take out what you need, then replace the slats. Make sure you purchase a well-made product though, since there is nothing as frustrating as trying to get out a poorly fitting slat!

Expense

With wooden compost bins you tend to get what you pay for. Good quality wood is more expensive than plastic, but you might be tempted by a 'bargain'. The cheaper kits are usually made from soft wood and can be quite badly made, making them frustrating to slot together. Hardwood bins are much sturdier and longer-lasting. You can choose either untreated wood, which is cheaper, or pressure-treated wood, which will add life (as well as expense) to the compost bin.

Pros

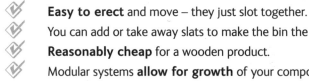

- **Easy to erect** and move – they just slot together.
- You can add or take away slats to make the bin the **right size** for your needs.
- **Reasonably cheap** for a wooden product.
- Modular systems **allow for growth** of your composting area and are suitable for hot composting.
- Treated timber can be guaranteed for many years and **lasts a long time**.

Cons

- Gaps between slats can mean that the compost **dries out** too quickly.
- **Weeds** can grow between the slats.
- Need **maintenance** such as wood preserver.
- **More expensive** than plastic bins.

Stacking or 'Beehive' Composters

Beehive composters are made from wood and, as their name suggests, they resemble beehives when completed. Unlike the slatted bins, the panels overlap so there are no gaps. Stacking compost bins are similar, but without the beehive shaping. Instead of graduated layers, they are all the same shape and size.

All Sorts of Shapes

There is no choice of shape with a beehive composter; they are designed to look like beehives, which makes them very attractive. Stacking bins literally stack on top of one another. Both styles are square which means that you can fit them into corners of your garden.

All Sorts of Sizes

You can build the compost bin up as and when you require by stacking layers on top
of one another. The lid should fit on any of the layers, so to begin with you might have
a short compost heap, but as you add more ingredients you simply stack another layer

up and put the lid on top of that one instead. You gradually build up the pile by adding ingredients and stacking another layer on the bin until it reaches the top. Sizes of this type of compost bin vary according to the manufacturer. You can buy beehive composters large enough for hot composting or small enough for a medium-sized garden. There are even baby models, which hold up to 200 litres (44 gallons) and are suitable for small gardens.

Water Retention

These types of compost bin have strong lids, so water retention is good. The best way to ensure the right levels of moisture in your compost bin is to pre-soak brown materials before adding them to the bin.

Keeping the Heat In

The closed sides and well fitting lid from this style of bin will contribute to keeping the heat in your compost heap. You can buy stacking bins large enough to hot compost.

Retrieving the Compost

Doors at the bottom of some models allow you easy access to the finished product. The most common way of retrieving the compost, however, is to lift the sections apart and take what you need. Other styles have a hinged lid, while others have front panels that are easily removed. Each make will vary slightly, so check out the accessibility before you make your purchase.

Tip

Remove the upper layers of this type of compost bin as the compost subsides and use these layers to begin your next batch.

Getting the Most from a Stacking Composter

One thing to bear in mind is that wood is much heavier than plastic. This is great in terms of durability, but might not suit everyone. Lifting stacks of wood isn't practical for some people and if the wood gets wet it can be even heavier and more awkward to move. Try lifting a couple of the stacks before purchasing one of these types of bin.

Expense

This style of composting bin is usually quite expensive. You are paying for the styling as well as the functionality. In addition, many of the beehive composters are available in a wide range of colours from pale pink to bright red; all of which you pay more for. Like slatted wooden bins, you get what you pay for. Look for hardwoods instead of soft. These will be more expensive but longer-lasting.

Pros

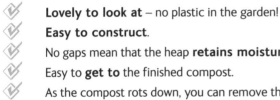

- **Lovely to look at** – no plastic in the garden!
- **Easy to construct**.
- No gaps mean that the heap **retains moisture**.
- Easy to **get to** the finished compost.
- As the compost rots down, you can remove the top layers of the bin and start a **new heap** somewhere else.
- They do not suffer **ultraviolet sun damage** like plastic can.

Cons

- **Expensive**.
- Wood needs to be **maintained**.
- Can be subject to **rotting**, especially soft wood.

Look out for

Buy one made from wood that is from a sustainable forest.

Tumblers

Tumbling composters take the strain out of turning and aerating the heap. They are a large plastic bin with a lid that rotates on a steel frame or moulded base. This allows complete mixing of ingredients, which helps aeration. This type of bin sounds like the perfect solution to the time-poor gardener, but is it? Tumbling bins can only take a small amount of raw ingredients and they usually need an activator. They are not open to the elements; they are completely enclosed, which has both good and bad points.

All Sorts of Shapes

There are three main types of tumbling composter – those that sit on a moulded base, those on an A-frame and those that are turned by a crank handle. They are all cylindrical to allow for rotation.

All Sorts of Sizes

Bins on a moulded base do not require any assembly. They take around 200 litres (44 gallons) of waste and are constructed from plastic. Those on a frame require simple home construction. The smallest size is around 150 litres (34 gallons), which is great for those with a small garden. Larger sizes go up to around 340 litres (75 gallons). These bins are usually made from plastic and the frame is made from steel. Those with a crank handle are the more robust and require two people to construct them safely and easily. They can take up to 650 litres (148 gallons) of composting material at one time. They are usually constructed from steel.

Portable

Most tumbling composters come with wheels, making them totally portable. You can keep yours close to your house when you want to walk out with vegetable peelings and wheel it to your vegetable beds when you're ready to spread your compost.

Water Retention

Depending on the construction, some bins have small holes for aeration, whereas others are completely enclosed. With either type, water retention is pretty good. These bins sell themselves on the fact that they are able to deal with large amounts of grass clippings, but it's better to get the right C:N by adding shredded cardboard or paper to maximize your chance of success.

Aerating

Many people are put off composting because of the effort involved in turning the ingredients. Using a tumbling bin means that aerating your compost is simple. When it is getting full, a tumbling bin can be heavy to move and rotate successfully. But when only half full, even the kids can get involved, which is a great way to introduce them to composting. When tumbling composters are too full, a rocking action will suffice; you don't need to turn them a complete 360 degrees to aerate successfully.

Keeping the Heat In

In order to successfully turn and mix the contents, there needs to be air space in the composter. This means that it is prone to losing heat. In order to compensate for this, aeration is made simple. What you lose in air space, you make up for with tumbling! Some models are insulated so that you can still make good compost in colder weather.

Tip

The benefit of a totally enclosed bin is that nothing can get in unless you put it in! That means no rats, other vermin or wasps.

Retrieving the Compost

Retrieving the compost is simple with some models. They are on a high frame so that you can wheel a barrow underneath the bin, open the door and the compost can be deposited straight into the barrow beneath. Others have a screw-on lid that you will need to remove before forking out the compost or tipping it out onto the ground. Bear in mind that some styles are over 1 m (3 ft) tall, so forking out the ingredients is pretty impossible; you will need someone to help you tip it!

Getting the Most from a Tumbling Composter

The downside to a tumbling composter is that you won't get worms or other beneficial beasties in there. You need worms to finish off the composting process so you'll have to add them. Adding a layer of good compost or garden soil will do the trick and don't forget about natural activators such as nettles and comfrey mentioned in previous chapters (see page 86). Tumbling composters are great for managing more greens than usual. However, if you have too many fine greens, such as fresh grass clippings, they can just roll into a smelly ball. This is not good for a gardener who produces more grass clippings than anything else. You'll need to break these clumps up with a small hand rake or similar. In addition, this type of composting bin requires that you shred all browns as finely as possible.

Expense

A tumbling bin requires an expensive outlay, but many people feel that the benefit of not needing to aerate the pile in the traditional way is worthwhile. Most bins come with a guarantee of around 5 years.

Pros

- Helpful if **space is limited** but you need room to tumble it!
- Great way to get **children** involved with composting.
- Extremely **mobile**.
- Aerating becomes a **fun activity** rather than a chore.
- **Quick** to produce compost – some companies claim it takes just 14 days.

Cons

- Can be **heavy** to turn when full.
- Can only process a **small amount** of raw ingredients at once.
- Prone to **losing heat**.
- Like a washing machine after a fast spin, the contents of a tumbling compost bin can **collect at one end** making it hard to rotate
- You need to be **committed** to using one properly. These bins need regular and frequent turning in order to produce good compost.

Look out for

Some models have a bar running through the middle to break up ingredients – if you have a lot of grass clippings this is useful to prevent clumping.

Open Heaps

An open heap is the traditional way of composting. Long before bins were on the market, everyone had a pile in a corner of their garden for kitchen and garden waste.

All Sorts of Shapes

Well, a heap is a heap! They are prone to spreading sideways so are not the neatest of composting methods, but they are functional and simple to put together.

All Sorts of Sizes

The beauty of an open heap is that you are not bound by size. It can be as small or large as you need. If you start off as a weekend gardener and don't produce many kitchen peelings or much garden waste then you can begin with a small heap. As your gardening skills grow, you can increase the size of the heap easily.

Water Retention

The main issue with an open heap is keeping the rainwater out. Ideally you would cover the heap with a tarpaulin or similar to keep moisture in and the rain out. Too much rain will not only make the heap too wet, but might leach valuable nutrients from the compost. Conversely, the surface ingredients on an open heap can dry out, especially on windy days. Rectify this by using a cover and mixing the ingredients well so that the materials on the outside get to the middle of the pile.

Keeping the Heat In

Surprisingly, open heaps are only slightly more prone to losing heat than enclosed ones. A large heap will retain the heat well and open heaps are suitable for hot composting. You can keep the heap insulated with a cover to maximize heat retention. Aerating an open heap is simple; you fork the contents from one area to another, mix them up and put them back.

Retrieving the Compost

Retrieving the compost couldn't be easier! You just fork out what you need into a wheelbarrow and take it away. It's also easy to see when the compost is finished in an open heap – you can take a peek at the bottom layers as often as you wish.

Getting the Most from an Open Heap

Open heaps are the most traditional type of heap. The contents can decompose as quickly as those in an enclosed bin if you have a good mix of organic matter. Open heaps provide the best conditions for attracting beneficial microorganisms because they are completely open.

> **Tip**
> Choose a well-sheltered site for an open heap and have covers on hand for wet or windy days.

Expense

It couldn't be cheaper! There are no materials required for setting up an open heap and you can construct a cover for nothing from an old piece of plastic sheeting or carpet. Members of www.freecycle.org frequently offer old pieces of carpet for exactly this purpose.

Pros

 You can make your heap exactly the **size** you want.

 Ideal for **hot composting**.

 Easy to **fork out** the finished compost.

 Easy to **aerate**.

 Very **cheap**!

Cons

 Will need **protecting** from heavy rainfall.

 Weed seeds can blow into an open compost area.

 Contents can get **scattered** by high winds or animals.

 Can look **messy**.

 In some areas they are **not suitable** due to animals and vermin.

Look Out For

Keep an eye out for suitable materials you can use to cover your heap.

DIY

One of the greenest ways to make your own compost bin is from scrap materials. Perhaps you have some offcuts of wood from a recent project, left over breeze blocks or bricks or access to some metal or wire. Some people even stack up old tyres and use those!

Have you Thought Of?

Composting can be a fun, sociable experience where you share ideas and resources between friends.

All Sorts of Shapes and Sizes

The shape and size of your bin is only limited by your imagination and the range of materials available to you. In this section you will read about using pallets, wire, straw, tyres, bags and boxes. But this is only the tip of the iceberg. If you look around your home, you'll probably see a huge range of materials that could be used for making a compost bin.

Pallets

Many people make compost bins from pallets. These are often available for free, but can have large gaps between the slats, which means that the ingredients on the outside of your bin can dry out and not decompose. Try lining them with something to fill the gaps, such as cardboard, which will eventually rot down into the compost. You can make a great base by getting hold of five pallets and using one as a floor. You can make access to the finished compost easier by making the front pallet a door by using hinges. If children will be using this compost heap, you'll need to sand down any rough edges.

Wire

Chicken wire or fencing wire makes a good material for a compost bin. Drive four wooden posts into the ground and fix the wire to them in a square or circle – whichever is easier. This will need lining with cardboard for insulation. You'll need to use much smaller wire than you think. A rat, for instance, can get through tiny gaps in the mesh and you don't want your compost ingredients falling out through the sides.

Tip

Look out for suitable free materials advertised locally. You might be able to gather enough materials to make a three-part system for nothing!

Straw

If you have room in your garden and access to straw bales then these make an excellent construction material for a compost heap. They provide great insulation and will eventually become part of the compost itself. They are ideal for hot composting and fit in with the landscape because they are a natural material. Straw might not be ideal in a very hot, dry climate due to fire risks.

Tyres

Many people use a stack of old tyres to grow their potatoes in, so why not use them for compost? Like stackable compost bins, you can add another tyre as your compost grows then take them off to retrieve the finished compost and begin another heap. Purists might be concerned about chemicals in tyres, but some say that tyres are inert and safe; you need to decide for yourself. A drawback to using tyres is that raw ingredients can get stuck in the moulding of the tyres, which is hard to scrape out. A benefit to using tyres is that they get incredibly hot in the sun, helping to speed up the composting process. You might find that you need to add more water to the heap to compensate for this.

Boxes

You might find yourself the proud owner of an enormous cardboard box – the type that office chairs or gas boilers arrive in. If you do, why not use it as a makeshift compost heap? Open out the bottom, fix it to the ground with some bricks or similar heavy objects and start adding your organic material. Keep the box covered with a piece of tarpaulin to protect it from driving wind and eventually the entire thing will make finished compost. This is suitable for spring or summer, but would probably not work during a wet or cold season.

Bags

The other item that people regularly find themselves with is builders' merchants' bulk bags. These are used to deliver sand or stone and are often non-returnable. Secure each side with a stake and use it to fill with your raw ingredients.

Pros

 Cost – these can be free!

 Made to measure, you can design your bin to fit wherever you want.

 Personal **satisfaction** from creating your own compost bin.

 Can grow or be **adapted** to suit your needs.

 Very **ecofriendly** if you reuse materials destined for the landfill.

Cons

- **Time consuming** to make your own bin.
- Needs **maintenance** if made from wood.
- Can look 'rustic', which is not the look everybody wants.
- Not always easy to get the **finished compost** out – consider this when you design your bin.
- It is not worth the **time and expense** of making a compost heap from wood unless you have access to free scrap wood or a good supply of reasonably priced timber.

Trench Composting

With trench composting you dig a trench in your soil, add your composting ingredients and cover it all over. Obviously there is not much oxygen in there, so you rely on natural decomposition processes to do the work, which takes time. This method is used on a site where you will plant crops like runner beans, peas, courgettes and pumpkins. To do trench composting, you dig the trench in the autumn wherever you will want to plant your crops in the spring. Fill the trench with alternate layers of kitchen waste and good soil. Once it is full, you cover the compost with soil and leave it.

All Sorts of Shapes

Trench composting is done in long, thin trenches in a space you can leave fallow for a while or where you plan to plant crops.

All Sorts of Sizes

You have complete control over the size of the trench. The size will depend on your space and the amount of material you have to compost.

Water Retention

Water retention is not usually an issue with trench composting, as everything is kept moist underground. All the bacteria and worms in the soil will have direct access to the raw ingredients too, so you literally leave nature to do its work. In sandy soils, lining the trench with cardboard is a good idea to prevent moisture loss.

Tip

Put a couple of markers in the soil at either end of your trench so that you can find it in six months' time!

Keeping the Heat In

Heat retention is not an issue with trench composting. The ground keeps everything warm, unless, of course, you live in an area prone to hard frosts.

Retrieving the Compost

With trench composting you don't retrieve the compost; you make it in situ. The compost is left in place and you plant crops on top of it.

Getting the Most From Trench Composting

Once the trench has been dug, filled and covered over there is nothing more for you to do. You can relax and let everything take care of itself until you are ready to plant over it again.

Expense

There is no financial expense, but you do need to be able to leave areas of your land fallow for a few months. This means that trench composting is really only suitable for those with large gardens and is no good if you only have a lawn, patio or flower borders.

Pros

 No cost.

 Minimal effort once the trench is dug.

 Nothing to look at – everything is underground.

Cons

 Takes a **long time** for raw ingredients to completely decompose.

 Only any good for those with **excess land**.

 It's a bit like a glorified **landfill**!

 Can take **nitrogen** from the soil, so leave plenty of time for it to decompose before planting over it.

 Depending on where you live, trenches may be dug up by **animals**.

Composting Systems

Now that you have determined the type of composting bin you are going to use, there are a few more factors to consider. You need to select the right sized bin, determine where to put it, how many you need and, if you have a particularly small or large garden, you might have special requirements. This section covers all that and more!

Selecting the Right Size of Compost Bin

It's important to choose the right size of compost bin for your needs. This will be determined predominantly by the size of your garden and how much waste you want to put into it. If you want to hot compost, you will need a large enough bin – a minimum of 1m (3 ft) long, by 1m (3 ft) wide, by 1m (3 ft) high.

What Size of Bin Does My Household Need?

It is initially quite difficult to choose a size of bin because each household produces a different amount of waste and has a different size of garden. As a very rough guide, the minimum sized composting bin for a family of 2 adults and 1 child with a small to medium garden would be 330 litres (73 gallons). For the same family with a larger garden, you would probably need two 330 litre (73 gallon) bins. For a two-person household with a small garden, around 250 litres (55 gallons) would be the minimum size.

Other Factors

The size of your lawn is an important factor to take into consideration. In the summer months, for example, lawn clippings can make up the majority of your waste. When you consider that you need to match the volume of grass cuttings with denser brown materials, such as cardboard or paper, you will ideally want a bin that can take all of this in one go.

Positioning Your Compost Bin

You'll need to think about where to put your bin. If your garden is small, perhaps you do not want to look out onto an ugly plastic bin. Neither will you want an untidy, sprawling heap. You can enjoy the best of both worlds by using some screening such as a trellis or climbing plant. Your heap needs to be somewhere unobtrusive, but not in a damp or heavily shaded corner. Ideally you will choose a level, well-sheltered, sunny spot.

The Best Place

The best place to put a compost heap is on well-drained, bare soil or grass, where microorganisms can find their way into your bin easily. You also need to make composting as practical for yourself as possible. The bin needs to be close enough to your house for taking out kitchen peelings and accessible for your garden when you want to use the finished compost.

Away from the Elements

Although direct sun will warm the heap up considerably, if the compost pile or bin is too small it can dry out the ingredients, which slows down the decomposition rate. The more wind and sun the pile is exposed to, the more water it will need. A compost heap needs to be protected from heavy rain. This is easily done in a compost bin with a lid, such as moulded plastic ones, but if you make your own you will need to make provision for this with an old piece of carpet, corrugated metal or plastic.

Trees

Locating the pile too close to trees can create problems as roots may grow into the bottom of the pile and make turning and handling the compost difficult. In an open pile, under trees, you might get too many leaves falling into it.

Water

Another consideration is water. There may be occasions when you need to add water to your compost pile. Do you have a source of water nearby, such as a water butt with a hosepipe attached, or will it be a difficult task to carry water to your compost pile?

Access

You need to be able to get to your bin easily. It might look better pushed between walls, fences or trees, but will you actually be able to get to it? And if you have wooden fences will they rot quicker without good airflow around them?

Recap

 If possible, site your bin on **bare soil** or grass.

 Ensure the bin is **accessible** – easy to get to and easy to use.

 Choose a **sunny, well-sheltered** spot.

 Keep your bin **covered** to protect from high winds and rain.

 Although it might look better, be wary of placing your compost heap **under trees**.

Do you have a source of **water** handy in case your compost pile dries out?

Number of Bins

The number of bins you have is dependant on your time commitments, garden space and the amount of waste you create. Having more than one bin is an advantage for a continual supply of compost, but it is not essential. If you are composting solely as a means of reducing your kitchen and garden waste to landfill and you won't be using much of the finished product around your garden, then one bin is sufficient. You can add to it as and when you have raw ingredients and it will gradually rot down into useable compost.

When More is Better

Two compost bins can be useful. This gives you the opportunity to be 'cooking' one batch (i.e. leaving well alone) while you are adding new ingredients to the other. Finished compost can be stored in old bags for a while or used up straight away. A stacking compost system allows you to create two compost bins with maximum flexibility.

Compost All Year Round

Having three bins is wonderful if you have the room. Ideally, one will be full of finished compost that you can use, another will be 'cooking' and the other will be being added to. This gives you virtually a year-round supply of compost, which is great for the avid gardener. Clearly compost bins take up room and need to be filled, so there is no point having more than you can site or use at once.

Recap

 The **number of bins** you have depends on your time, space and amount of waste materials.

 One bin is sufficient for a small household with a small garden.

 Two bins mean that you can be cooking one batch of compost while adding to the next.

 Three bins mean you get virtually a year-round supply of compost.

Composting in a Large Garden

If you have a large garden then a three-part composting system is ideal. This will maximize your chances of having a continual supply of compost for all your needs. A large garden has the advantage of space to site bins in easily accessible but out-of-the-way locations. It will also provide plenty of materials to fill the bins with. In a large garden, you can benefit from hot (active) composting and you are not limited in the type of bin you choose. You can even decide to have heaps if you prefer because of the amount of space you have.

Composting in a Small Garden

Even if you don't have a stately home with rambling gardens, you can still compost. In fact, composting can be done in the tiniest of spaces. There are all sorts of compost bins available that are suitable for all garden sizes. If you are living on your own and don't have a lawn, then a small, lightweight moulded plastic bin is perfect. The finished contents can be used for plant pots if you don't have beds.

Liquid Gold

If you choose a small plastic bin, try and get one where it is easy to collect the liquid run-off. This will provide you with a nutrient-rich fertilizer for container plants, so that you can maximize the benefits of your composting efforts.

Indoor Composting

If you don't have a garden then there is no need to feel left out. There are still ways for you to compost! You can still benefit from reduced landfill waste (this makes your dustbin lighter to take to the kerbside for collection and may reduce fees if you live in an area where you pay by weight) and free food for house plants, hanging baskets and containers. It sounds a bit of a contradiction to talk of indoor composting, but there are successful methods.

Inside, Outside

If you have a tiny patch of garden, but nowhere to put a compost bin outside you can put one in a shed, garage or porch. A tumbling composter that will not leak any fluid is ideal for this type of situation. Remember that you will need to introduce microorganisms and some of your wiggly friends.

Wormeries

If you have no outdoor land then you can keep a wormery indoors for your kitchen waste and scrap paper. You will not get much compost, but you will get valuable 'liquid gold', which is a wonderful plant fertilizer. You can use this in containers and for house plants. Read more about wormeries in the chapter Other Types of Composting (see page 136).

Bokashi Bins

If you don't have room for a wormery indoors then there is still another option! A bokashi bin or kitchen composter sits on your kitchen work surface and will make quick work of your kitchen waste including cooked food scraps, meat, fish and bones.

Community Spirit

Alternatively, why not get involved with a community garden and take your food scraps there to be composted? If you live in an apartment, you might be able to arrange a wormery between a few of you. It's a great way to get to know your neighbours and share a common and valuable interest.

HAve you Thought Of?

Composting is not just for people with gardens – there are suitable systems for people who live in apartments too.

Recap

- The **site** of your bin is important – choose a sunny, well-sheltered spot with good access.
- **How many** compost bins do you need? This will depend on your time, space and the availability of raw materials.
- A **large garden** will benefit from a three-part system to ensure a continual supply of compost.
- Someone with a **small garden** and little time for composting can benefit from a small, moulded plastic bin.
- If you **don't have a garden**, then a shed, garage or porch could be the ideal place for a compost bin. A tumbling composter would be ideal.
- If you live in an **apartment**, you can choose between a wormery and a bokashi bin.

Checklist

☑ Determine **what size** of bin or heap you need – think about the volume of materials you will be composting and the available space in your garden.

☑ **Set a budget** for your compost bin and start looking at available options.

☑ If you are going to make your own compost bin, start **gathering materials**.

☑ **Choose a location** for your bin – close enough to your house for filling, but convenient for where you want to use your finished compost.

☑ Look at the **pros and cons** for each type of compost bin – which one suits your needs? Moulded plastic, self-assembly plastic, wooden slats, stacking, tumbler, open heap or DIY?

☑ **How many** bins do you need? Do you have the room and the raw materials for them?

☑ Is **trench composting** a good option for you? (Perhaps so if you only want to plant crops at a certain point in the year and you have plenty of space!)

☑ Do you need to look at **smaller options** such as a wormery or a bokashi bin?

☑ Don't forget to **take advantage** of the liquid run off by choosing an appropriate bin.

Other Types of Composting

Vermicomposting

A regular compost heap is not the only way to produce compost to feed your soil. If your household only produces kitchen waste and does not have any garden waste then you can still compost. Vermicomposting (worm composting) involves the use of special types of worm that digest and recycle your kitchen waste into worm castings and liquid fertilizer. The worms live in a wormery.

What Is a Wormery?

The simplest type of wormery is made up of different layers. The bottom layer catches the valuable liquid fertilizer – many wormeries come with a tap to siphon this off. The next layer up contains the worms' bedding, made from soaked coir or newspaper. Subsequent layers contain the food you feed to the worms. The worms burrow up through the layers to find food.

How a Wormery Works

In a stacking wormery, the bottom layer is gradually filled with vermicompost, ready to be used, the middle layer is being digested by the worms, and is half ready, and the top layer is where you add new waste. Complete kits that include everything you need, including the worms, can be bought from garden centres and specialist online stores. A beginner's kit will come with around 500 g worms.

Which Type of Worm Do I Use?

You cannot simply dig up earthworms from someone's garden for a successful wormery. The types of worm required for a wormery are called red worms (or tiger or brandling). These are much smaller than earthworms and require a different diet. They are available from online suppliers, gardening stores and some angling shops.

Where Can I Keep My Wormery?

The wormery can be sited wherever is convenient – in a garage or shed, on a balcony, on a porch or even in the kitchen. Worms like cool, damp places, so don't put your wormery in direct sunlight or you might have some casualties to deal with. Activity will slow down if the worms get too cold, so bear this in mind if you live in a cold climate and plan to keep your wormery outside. You can insulate the wormery with straw or an old piece of carpet. Wormeries are ideal for people with no garden at all who want to reduce their household waste!

Do I Have to Keep Replacing Dead Worms?

If conditions are favourable, the worms will thrive and breed. They can breed every couple of weeks. Don't worry though; you won't be overrun with worms – they will self-regulate to make the most of the food source and space. They are clever creatures! If all goes well, you will buy your initial batch of worms and not need to replace them.

Why Should I Bother Vermicomposting?

Worms make short work of your kitchen waste – these hungry creatures can eat up to half their own body weight of waste every day! Not only will you reduce your landfill waste, using a wormery also means that at the end of their meal, your worms will leave you with a superb present – top quality compost! Wormeries are useful for people with limited space, no garden or for those who do not have the time or energy to manage traditional garden composting. They are self-contained and there is little chance of smells, spillage or escape.

Nutrient-rich Compost

The resulting worm casts from your wormery are nutrient-rich; far richer than anything you will get from your compost heap! Plants and vegetable seedlings love worm casts and a little goes a long way. The worm castings can be dug into soil for improving its structure, increasing water retention and enhancing plant growth. You can add worm casts to containers used for house plants or apply it as mulch and it is suitable for any container gardening. In addition, you can collect a wonderful fertilizing liquid from the bottom layer that can be diluted 10 times with water and used as a general-purpose plant feed. Tomatoes drink this up!

How Long Does It Take to Produce Compost?

Getting compost from your wormery doesn't take as long as you might expect. The liquid fertilizer can be siphoned off quite quickly in some instances; especially if you feed a lot of fruit and vegetable peelings, as these have a high water content. Within a few months, you'll be gathering your first batch of worm casts. It will be a small amount, but it is so rich that you will need to mix it with soil or potting compost before use.

What About Going on Holiday?

Once your wormery is well established and you know how much your worms are eating, you can put some food in the top layer and leave them for up to a month unattended. They don't need any special care. Just make sure the temperature is stable before you leave so that the worms will not be subjected to any significant temperature fluctuations.

What Can I Feed the Worms?

You'll be amazed by the variety of foods your worms will eat. You can feed them all sorts of natural things including:

- Cooked vegetable leftovers such as bits of bread, pasta, cereal, cakes.
- Raw fruit and vegetable peelings.
- Cardboard or paper, shredded and soaked in water.
- Human hair or animal fur.
- Tea leaves and coffee grounds.
- Eggshells (not the contents).
- Flowers.
- Vacuum cleaner contents, as long as you have natural flooring.

What Must I Not Feed the Worms?

You must not put anything synthetic in your wormery. They cannot, for instance, eat plastics. Other items you cannot feed them are:

- Too much citrus. A little is ok.
- Paper with shiny ink.
- Meat, fish or bones.
- Some worms don't like potato peelings, onions or garlic.
- Dairy.

More About Feeding

Feed your worms little and often. If you put too much waste in there, it will start to rot before the worms can get through it. This will result in bad smells and can kill the worms. If your wormery does start to smell, take out any rotting food and add some damp, shredded cardboard. About 40 per cent of the volume of the food you give your worms should be made up of cardboard or paper to prevent the wormery becoming too wet. You need it damp but not wet, otherwise it can attract fruit flies. It is a good idea to cover food peelings and scraps with a little paper to prevent attracting flies anyway.

Tip

Crushed eggshells can prevent the environment becoming overly acidic.

When Is the Vermicompost Ready?

The worms will keep burrowing upwards in search of food. When most of them are in the top layer of your wormery you can take the compost from the bottom layer. Vermicompost is ready when there are no uneaten bits of food or bedding in the mix. It will no longer bear any resemblance to the original raw materials. The liquid is ready more quickly and you can frequently siphon this off, dilute it and use it on your plants. It is advisable to check the pH of the liquid before using, as it will vary tremendously according to the ingredients you put into your wormery.

Can I Speed up the Process?

After a period of time you will get used to the amount of food your worms can eat. You need to start small, monitor how much they get through and, as the worms breed, you'll find they eat more. The result is that you will get more compost in a shorter period of time. You cannot make the process happen quicker by feeding the worms more than they can eat. This is more likely to result in rotting food and unhappy worms.

Pros

Ideal for those with **limited space** – wormeries can be set up inside the home.

Free, nutrient-rich **plant food**.

No smell.

Vermicomposting can create compost **all year round**.

Cons

Only processes a small amount of **kitchen waste** – no good for large families.

Only get a small amount of **compost** at the end (although it is rich in nutrients).

Can be **expensive** to set up.

Recap

Vermicomposting uses a **special type of worm** to produce rich compost and plant food from kitchen waste.

Vermicomposting is useful for **small households** without garden waste.

Start feeding **little and often** so you can establish your worms' appetite!

Keep the worms **warm** enough in winter and **cool** in the summer.

Leaf Mould

If your garden produces a lot of leaves in the autumn, then composting them into leaf mould is better than trying to put them all in your compost bin. Like grass clippings, lots of leaves take up a large volume, plus they can mat together and prevent air getting into your compost heap. Some leaves, like oak leaves, can take a long time to decompose and adding them to a regular compost heap slows down the process.

What Is Leaf Mould?

Leaf mould is a special type of compost made just from leaves. Unlike traditional composting, which involves a wide range of ingredients, only leaves are used to make leaf mould. Don't worry about the word mould; it has nothing to do with a seething mass of fungi! Leaf mould is not high in nutrients, but is an excellent soil conditioner.

How Long Does It Take to Make Leaf Mould?

Leaves are high in carbon and can take a long time to decompose in a compost heap. In addition, they are rotted down by the cool, slow action of fungi, rather than the hot conditions that a compost heap requires. This is why too many leaves in your compost heap can slow the process and you may find leaves in the finished product that have not fully decomposed. Separating leaves and making leaf mould will prevent them slowing down your composting. Leaf mould can take a few years to develop, especially if the trees you have access to are predominantly oak, beech or evergreens, but for the amount of work involved, it is worth it.

Why Should I Bother Making Leaf Mould?

Leaf mould is worth waiting for! It is an excellent soil improver and conditioner and can be used for potting. Leaf mould improves moisture retention in sandy soils and helps drainage in heavy clay soils. It is rich in microorganisms that can prevent diseases. Leaf mould can be used as mulch to suppress weeds, retain moisture, prevent soil erosion and protect seeds during the winter time. Leaf mould can be used virtually anywhere in the garden at any time of the year. Vegetables, fruits and flowers will all benefit. There is no specialist equipment required, so it's totally free.

How to Make Leaf Mould

Leaf mould is made in the autumn when all the leaves fall from the trees. If possible, gather the fallen leaves after rain to ensure good water content, as this will help speed up the initial decomposition. It is preferable to shred the leaves and break them down into tiny pieces. An easy way to do this is to mow them. If it is not possible to gather the leaves after rain, then water them as you layer them into your container. You don't need to add anything else; wet leaves are all you need.

Making Leaf Mould in a Large Garden

In a large garden, with lots of trees, you will need to make or buy a suitable container to store your leaves to stop them blowing away. The best type is something constructed from fine wire or mesh. Unlike composting, heat retention is not an issue so you can use whatever you have to hand. If you have an old compost bin lying around, then use that. Cover the collected leaves with an old piece of carpet. As with the hot composting method, the best size of container for making leaf mould is 1 m (3 ft) cubed. This helps to retain moisture in the pile. Once you have filled your container, leave it to work. Just check every now and again that the surface is not too dry and water if necessary.

Tip

Builders' merchants' bulk bags make ideal containers for making leaf mould.

Making Leaf Mould in a Small Garden

If you have a small garden but with a few trees, you can still benefit from leaf mould. The easiest way is to put a few air holes in a black plastic bag, fill it with wet leaves and tie the top.

When Is It Ready?

After a year or so, the leaf mould can be used as mulch for putting around shrubs and vegetables. You can use it to cover bare soil during the winter or as a soil improver when sowing and planting. At this stage the leaves have started to rot and will crumble easily in your hand but will still be recognizable. If you leave the leaf mould for two years or more, it can be used as potting compost. It is carbon-rich and many seeds love it. At this stage it is rich, dark, fine, soft and crumbly and it smells like a forest floor.

Can I Speed up the Process?

Even though leaf mould is usually made from one ingredient, the addition of grass clippings in the spring following the autumn you begin the pile (i.e. six months later) will help to speed up the process. You will not get pure leaf mould like this however, it will be a cross between compost and leaf mould. Adding a fine layer of garden soil or good quality compost between layers of leaves is another way to speed up the process.

Pros

 Simple to make – requires little attention and set up.

 Free to make.

 Saves using peat-based compost.

 Reduces the number of bonfires you need to have.

 Great for soil.

 Reduces the amount of **watering** you need to do if it is used as a mulch or soil improver.

Cons

 Can be **time-consuming** to gather the leaves.

 Can look **messy** in a small garden.

 Timing is important – you need to gather the leaves soon after falling otherwise you might disturb wildlife that make their homes in leaf piles.

Recap

 Leaf mould is a special type of compost made just from leaves.

It is better to compost leaves separately from your compost heap because they require **different conditions** to decompose.

Leaf mould can take **two years** or more to complete.

It is an excellent **soil improver** and helps retain moisture, so well worth doing.

No specialist equipment is required.

Green Johanna

Green Johanna may well sound like the name of an ecofriendly woman, but it's actually a specific type of composter. Designed in Sweden, the Green Johanna is a closed hot-composting container designed to break down organic materials quickly and efficiently. The Green Johanna is ideal for households who wish to compost both kitchen and garden waste, including meat and fish. It is a compromise between a compost bin and a digester and is ideal for people who like the idea of hot composting, but don't feel confident enough (or have enough raw materials) for the traditional method.

What Is a Green Johanna?

A Green Johanna is a plastic, cone-shaped bin with small holes in the base. These allow good ventilation and access for worms, but are too small for rats to enter. They are similar in appearance to a plastic compost bin. There is a collection hatch at the bottom for retrieving finished compost and a lid to keep the heat in. For daily temperatures of below 5°C (41°F), the Green Johanna comes with an insulation jacket to help retain the temperature needed for composting to continue. When daily temperatures reach up to 10°C (50°F) take the jacket off, otherwise you can burn the compost and kill the microorganisms. The design is such that it ensures a hot compost environment, regardless of the amount going in or the effort taken to turn the ingredients.

Site Your Green Johanna

Like a regular compost bin, a Green Johanna should be placed on bare soil or grass so that worms and microorganisms can find their way in. Unlike a regular compost bin, this type of composter should be in a well-sheltered position, such as the corner of your garden or under a tree. They do not do well in direct sunlight; the more shaded the better.

Layering a Green Johanna

As with traditional composting methods, the ingredients added to a Green Johanna need to be layered to maintain a good carbon to nitrogen ratio and to ensure rapid decomposition. In a similar way to traditional composting, the first layer should be something that helps the composter to drain – small twigs are ideal. Make the first layer around 15 cm (6 in). The next layer should be shredded garden waste, followed by good quality compost or soil. After that you can begin to add your kitchen waste.

What Can I Compost in a Green Johanna?

- Bread
- Coffee grounds and filters
- Dairy
- Eggshells
- Grass clippings
- Leaves
- Meat, fish and bones

- Sawdust
- Shredded paper and cardboard
- Tea bags
- Twigs, broken into small pieces
- Vegetable and fruit peelings
- Weeds

Tip

Keep a caddy on your kitchen work surface for your kitchen waste and empty it with a layer of browns into the Green Johanna daily.

Layering is Important

When you do traditional composting, once you have a feel for the right ratio of green materials to browns, you can stop layering and just put the raw ingredients in the compost bin. With a Green Johanna, good layering is an important part of the process to ensure successful composting. The best ratio for a Green Johanna is one part garden waste or other browns to two parts kitchen waste. Shredding the ingredients as finely as possible and layering loosely in thin layers helps. Always finish with a layer of browns.

Aerating

As with traditional composting, the Green Johanna needs a good air supply. This type of composter needs to be aerated *every time* you add new ingredients. A special stirring stick comes with each Green Johanna specifically for this job. You use it to aerate the top 15 cm (6 in) of the compost. This is not as difficult as turning a conventional compost heap and only takes a few moments.

How Long Before I Get Some Compost?

Your compost should be ready in around six months. It will look, smell and feel just like regular compost – dark, crumbly and with an earthy smell. It is retrieved from a hatch at the bottom of the cone, which means you can take out the finished compost and leave the other materials in there to continue the decomposition process. Use the compost on vegetable patches or around bushes. Unfinished compost can be used as mulch.

Pros

 Can be used to compost **cooked food waste** including meat, fish and bones.

 Can be used to make compost **all year round**.

Cons

 Needs **daily attention** – adding new ingredients and aerating.

 Initial expense.

Recap

 A **Green Johanna** is a special type of hot composter.

A Green Johanna needs to be situated in a **shady**, **cool place**.

Layering is very important to ensure the decomposition process works.

Compost can be retrieved in around **six months**.

Green Cone

A Green Cone isn't strictly a composter, as you don't get any compost from it. It's technically known as a Food Waste Digester System. Unlike traditional composting, you do not add any garden waste to a Green Cone; it's purely for food waste. It is designed to accept biodegradable waste that would not be placed in a traditional composting unit. You can safely put cooked food, meat and dairy into it. A well functioning Green Cone can accept up to 1 kg (2 lb) of food waste every day and will help you to reduce the amount of food you send to the landfill.

Site Your Green Cone

A Green Cone needs to go in the sunniest place in your garden and must not be in the cold, dark or wet. It needs to be on bare soil or grass because the bottom part of the Green Cone (the basket) is installed beneath the surface of the earth. You need to dig a hole up to 1 m (3 ft) wide and 70 cm (2½ ft) deep for the basket. The base is filled with well-draining materials such as gravel, stones or small pieces of broken terracotta pots along with some of the dug out soil or good quality compost. The upper part of the Green Cone sits on top of the basket, level with the ground.

How Does a Green Cone Work?

The Green Cone consists of several parts. The basket is underground as mentioned above; microorganisms and worms migrate freely in and out of this basket to break down the waste. A double-walled solar cone sits on top of the basket and creates a heat trap of circulating air to encourage bacterial growth. In addition there is a removable lid. Take care to follow the manufacturer's instructions and install your Green Cone properly; it needs excellent drainage otherwise it will not work effectively.

How to Use Your Green Cone

The Green Cone is used solely for food and not for garden waste. You can add your food waste as and when, having collected it in your kitchen caddy. During long periods of cold weather you can add an accelerator powder, which is a mixture of natural bacteria, to keep the Green Cone working efficiently. No layering is needed; you just put everything in the Green Cone and leave it to decompose. There is no smell.

Safety Issues

The Green Cone has been designed with curious children in mind. It comes with a metal bar, which sits across the opening of the green cone. This prevents children from falling in. If you do not have children, or they are old enough not to explore, then you can remove the bar. Removing the bar makes emptying contents into the Green Cone easier.

What to Put in Your Green Cone

You can put virtually any type of food waste including:

 Fruit and vegetable peelings

 Dairy

 Crushed eggshells

 Meat, fish and bones

 Cooked food waste

 Tea bags

In addition, a Green Cone will deal with small amounts of animal faeces.

What Must Not Be Added

You cannot put other compostable materials into a Green Cone such as:

 Paper and cardboard
 Garden waste
 Sawdust

Remember, a Green Cone is for food waste and not garden waste. Neither can you add synthetics such as plastic.

How Do I Know My Green Cone Is Working?

If the Green Cone is working properly you will notice that your food waste is covered in a blue-grey fur – this indicates that all is well. If you do not notice this fur then you need to add some accelerator powder until the fur starts to appear.

Emptying a Green Cone

A well-functioning Green Cone will only need emptying every few years. There is no compost to gather; your food waste is converted into water, carbon dioxide and a small amount of residue. The residue can be dug into a suitable piece of ground, such as around ornamental plants. The base unit of the Green Cone is situated well below the level of the soil so rats are not a problem. The lack of maintenance and attention needed makes the Green Cone the ideal solution for those who are concerned about landfill waste and the environment but are not avid gardeners.

Pros

 Can deal with **cooked food waste**, which cannot be traditionally composted.
 No aerating, watering or **maintenance** required.
 No **layering** needed.
 No need to **feed daily** – as and when is fine.
 The design means that it will not attract **vermin**.

- Usually comes with a kitchen caddy and **accelerator powder**.
- Ideal if you do not want to deal with **compost**.

Cons

- Cannot deal with **garden waste**.
- May not work efficiently on **clay soil**.
- **Ongoing cost** from accelerator powder.
- **Installation** takes a lot of effort and needs to be done correctly.
- You do not benefit from an end product like **compost**.

Recap

- A **Green Cone** is a food digester that does not produce compost.
- It needs a **sunny location**.
- The base is **dug into the ground** and the main part sits on top.
- Accepts **all food waste** on an as-and-when basis, but no garden waste.
- Raw ingredients decompose and the resulting **liquid seeps away** into the surrounding soil harmlessly.

Bokashi Bins

A bokashi bin, sometimes referred to as a kitchen composter or EmPowered composting, is a method of intensive indoor composting. You can buy a start-up kit from various online suppliers consisting of two bokashi bins and a pack of effective microorganisms. Using a bokashi bin is not technically composting, it is a method of fermenting and it takes place anaerobically.

How to Use a Bokashi Bin

Ideally you have two bokashi bins, one of which you are using and the other which is fermenting your raw ingredients. The bins are small buckets with airtight lids and a small tap at the bottom – ideal for putting on your kitchen work surface. You fill your bucket with food scraps and peelings. On top of each layer you sprinkle over some specially formulated effective microorganisms (EM), commonly referred to as bokashi bran. The EM ferments and accelerates the breakdown of organic matter. You continue to place alternating layers of food and bokashi EM until the bin is full. Bokashi bins are small, so contents ferment better if you cut up any peelings into small pieces before adding them.

Bokashi Bran

Bokashi bran is a dry mixture of bran, molasses and effective microorganisms. Effective microorganisms are a mix of bacteria, yeasts and fungi, which work to speed up the composting process and prevent putrefaction. A well operating bokashi bin has a mild fermenting smell, a bit like sweet vinegar. Bokashi bran can be bought from various online suppliers and gardening stores.

Tip

Try pushing down each layer of food with a potato masher to try and exclude as much air as possible.

What to Put in a Bokashi Bin

You can put the following into a bokashi bin:

 Fruit and vegetable peelings

 Cooked food scraps

 Meat, fish and small bones

 Solid dairy products such as cheese
or butter

Crushed eggshells

 Well squeezed-out or dried tea bags and coffee grounds

 A small amount of shredded paper and cardboard such as the occasional tissue

Have you Thought Of?

It is estimated that the average household's rubbish is 19 per cent food waste; using a bokashi, food digester or wormery could reduce your waste dramatically.

What Not to Put in a Bokashi Bin

The following items should not be put into a bokashi bin:

 Garden waste

 Sawdust

 Synthetics

 Liquids such as milk or juice

When the Bokashi Bin Is Full

When the bokashi bin is full it is left to ferment for around 14 days. As with a wormery, you get a liquid run-off (bokashi juice), which can be siphoned from the tap. While one bin is fermenting, you can be filling the second to ensure a continual supply of bokashi compost.

How Do I Know When the Contents Are Ready?

Unlike with traditional compost, you do not rely on the earthy smell or broken-down appearance of the contents of your bokashi bin to signal when it is ready. Bokashi bins work by pickling the contents, so you will still recognize some of the contents. The actual breakdown of the waste happens a few weeks later once the fermented bokashi contents have been put on a compost heap or into the soil. The contents of your bokashi bin will still be recognizable and might be covered in a white, cotton-like mould. As long as they have a sweet/sour smell, not a putrid one, then they are ok!

Using Bokashi Juice

Bokashi juice can be diluted 100 times with water (it is very acidic) and used as plant food. In addition, bokashi juice is great for households on a septic tank system – just pour it down the drain to keep the system healthy. Do not store bokashi juice; use within 24 hours of draining from the bucket.

Using the Bokashi Bin Contents

The contents of a bokashi bin can be mixed into a regular compost heap where they help to accelerate the decomposition process. If you do not have your own compost bin, you may be able to donate them to a willing friend, community compost heap or school garden. Alternatively, you can bury bokashi contents by digging them into the soil. Digging bokashi compost into the soil acts as a soil conditioner and supplies microbes. You need to add it to the soil six weeks before planting. If you don't have a garden, then you can mix the bokashi contents with potting compost (one part bokashi to four parts compost is ideal) and use in a window box or containers. Again, leave for six weeks before planting. Some people put their bokashi contents into a wormery where the worms will continue the composting process.

Making the Most of Bokashi Bins

Bokashi bins are ideal for small households or those with no garden. Teamed with a wormery, you can use the bokashi to dispose of cooked food waste, meat and fish, and the wormery to deal with fruit and vegetable peelings.

Pros

- Works well with **other methods** of composting such as vermicomposting.
- Ideal for people with **limited space**; the bins sit on your kitchen work surface.
- Takes **cooked food waste** including meat, fish and small bones.
- Contents can help **activate** a traditional compost heap.
- Useful for ingredients like **citrus and onions**, which some worms don't like.

Cons

- Need to buy EM, so there is an **ongoing cost**.
- Need somewhere to **deposit the finished contents** as they still need to fully decompose.
- Can be an **expensive outlay**.
- Some people find the **smell** of the liquid and finished product offensive.

Recap

- Bokashi **bins** are a method of indoor composting.
- They are ideal for **leftover food** scraps.
- After adding new ingredients, sprinkle with a **layer of EM**.
- Fill the bin, seal and leave for two weeks to **ferment**.
- Bokashi juice can be **diluted 100 times** with water and used on plants.
- Fermented bokashi contents can be added to a **compost heap** or wormery or mixed into soil.

	Bokashi Bin	Green Cone	Green Johanna	Leaf Mould	Wormery
Bones	✓	✓	✓	X	X
Cooked food scraps	✓	✓	✓	X	✓
Dairy	✓	✓	✓	X	X
Eggshells	✓	✓	✓	X	✓
Grass clippings and garden waste	X	X	✓	A few	X
Leaves	X	X	✓	✓	X
Meat and fish	✓	✓	✓	X	X
Paper and cardboard	X	X	✓	X	✓
Raw fruit and vegetable peelings	✓	✓	✓	X	✓
Tea bags and coffee grounds	✓	✓	✓	X	✓

Checklist

- Consider the other methods of composting outlined in this chapter – is there one that **suits your lifestyle**?

- If you have trees in your garden, why not make **leaf mould** this year?

- Would a **Green Cone** or **Green Johanna** be better for your needs? Do you have the right location for one? A Green Johanna needs shade and a Green Cone needs full sun.

- Do you need to compost **garden waste**? If so, you'll need a Green Johanna.

- If you need an **indoor composting** method, look at the types of kitchen waste you create most of – fruit and vegetable peelings are better for a wormery, cooked food waste is better dealt with by a bokashi bin.

- Find out the prices of different **wormeries** and choose the best one for your household.

- Remember that a bokashi bin requires special **effective microorganisms**; shop around for the best deal.

- If you decide on a **bokashi bin**; do you have somewhere to deposit the finished contents?

Using
Compost

Using Compost

Now comes the fun part. You are about to be rewarded for all your time and energy, by getting to use your compost! There are plenty of places to use your compost; the most obvious is vegetable beds but trees, your lawn, seeds, flowers, containers and house plants will all benefit. Once you get used to using your compost you'll realise that you can never have enough of it.

A Few Cautions

There are a few cautions to bear in mind before using your home compost. These will ensure you get the most from your gardening experience:

 Ensure your compost is **fully cured** before using.

 Even though you can never have enough compost in your garden, there are some plants which **don't like very much** of it.

 Once your compost is ready it's better to use it up within **six months** or valuable nutrients might be lost.

 If you have **cats** in your garden, then keep your fine compost covered; cats love to use it for their toilet.

Ensure Your Compost Is Fully Cured Before Using

If your compost is not fully cured before using, it may still contain active bacteria. Once mixed into the soil, these can rob the earth of oxygen and nitrogen. As you'll remember, your compost heap requires oxygen to be active. If the decomposition process has not finished, the high level of microbial activity can pull oxygen from the surrounding soil, which can suffocate plant roots. In addition, immature compost will draw on soil nitrogen to assist the decomposition process. This can leave the area around the plant roots nitrogen-poor.

Rather than enhancing the growth of your plants, immature compost can burn plant roots and stunt, damage or even kill plants. Refer to the chapter How to Compost (see page 92) to check whether your compost is fully cured.

Some Plants Don't Like Compost!

Even though too much can never be enough when it comes to making compost, there are some plants that don't like rich soil. For instance, some herbs actually thrive in poor soil, so these should be given a wide berth when you're handing out your compost. You'll get used to the hungry feeders in your garden and you can always refer to a gardening book or website for specific advice.

Use Finished Compost Within Six Months

Use finished compost within six months or it may lose some of its nutrients through leaching. This isn't the end of the world, but it's a shame not to make the most of your hard work. Compost is still a good soil conditioner, regardless of its nutritional value, and will help to improve soil structure. Store finished compost away from rain, which can wash away the nutrients. Old plastic bags are ideal for this.

Watch Out For Cats!

Cats are clean creatures that will happily bury their faeces, but they can be lazy animals that will take the easy option if there is one. And who can blame them?! Fine, crumbly compost makes the perfect cat toilet; so if you don't want any unpleasant surprises when handling your compost, give some thought to where you will store your finished product. If it is already in a closed compost bin there won't be a problem, but open heaps are an invitation to furry friends. If you can't keep it covered, make sure you wear gloves when dealing with your compost.

The Wonders Of Compost

You've painstakingly attended to your compost for the past few months, maybe even years. Now everything is ready, but you have to ask yourself – what have you actually been making for the past year? What is the deal with compost? Why do gardeners rave about this brown crumbly stuff so much? Compost is a bit like a superfood, a tonic and a medicine for all your gardening needs. In short, compost:

- Maintains **healthy soil**.
- Helps improve **sick soil**.
- Makes plants more **resistant to disease**.
- Makes plants less prone to attack from **pests**.
- Improves soil **structure**.
- **Feeds plants**.
- **Suppresses weeds**.
- **Retains moisture** so that you can use less water.
- Can be used to **rejuvenate** old compost.
- Is a useful **mulch**.

Soil

As mentioned in the previous section, compost improves soil structure, suppresses weeds, can be used as mulch and most plants love it. Compost is the organic portion of the soil. A good, healthy soil needs around five per cent organic matter to support healthy plant life. Compost feeds the soil and the soil feeds your plants. You have to take more care of the soil than the plants! A sick plant is a symptom of something else – often poor soil. Take care of the soil by using some of your lovely compost and the soil will take care of your flowers, vegetables, house plants, herbs, trees and shrubs for you.

Soil Improver

Compost is invaluable for improving the texture and condition of your soil. Compost will create air pockets in heavy, clay soils to increase airflow, relieve compaction and help break up the soil. In sandy soil, compost will increase the nutrient- and water-retaining capabilities of the soil. Compost can hold its own weight in water, so if you want to get water down to your plant roots and hold it there, you need compost in your soil. To improve your soil, mix a 10–15 cm (4–6 in) layer of finished compost into the earth. Initially, you might need to dig this in, but after a couple of years you can put the compost on top of the soil in autumn and leave the worms and rain to do the mixing for you. Home compost can be used as a soil improver on all types of plant beds including those growing vegetables, flowers and ornamental shrubs.

Compost Feeds the Soil

Compost makes essential nutrients like nitrogen, potassium and a number of other minerals available for the plants to use. In addition, compost feeds the microbes in the soil. Remember, you're interested in feeding the soil, not the plants. It could be argued that microbial

Have you Thought Of?

How much money you might be saving by making your own compost instead of buying it?

population in the soil is far more important to the plant than fertilizer. Well-conditioned soil is easier for you to work with, as well as providing your plants with all the nutrients they need to thrive. Happy, healthy plants mean that you get higher fruit and vegetable yields and more beautiful plants and flowers to enjoy.

Mulch

Compost can be used as mulch. To mulch, you spread the compost on top of the soil around plants. You can use part-finished compost for this purpose. Mulching is done for many reasons including:

-    **Water** retention.
- Suppression of **weeds**.
- Adding **nutrients** to the soil.
- Maintaining soil **temperatures**.
- **Erosion** control.

Mulching is the baseline for good organic gardening. Spread a 3–8 cm (1–3 in) thick layer of compost around plants, trees or shrubs and leave it to break down. Don't, however, go right up to the plant stems or tree trunks. Repeat again later in the year if your soil needs a lot of conditioning. If you live in a climate with extremes of temperature, mulching can help protect your soil. Water plants thoroughly before mulching, apply the mulch and then water again.

Mulching For Weed Suppression

If you are using mulch as a weed suppressant, you'll need to spread it in layers of about 10–15 cm (4–6 in). You'll also notice that you can use much less water on your garden because you will have decreased the evaporation rate of your soil. Any weeds that grow from live seed weeds in the compost can be easily taken off with a hoe before they root.

Vegetables and Herbs

Compost is the most important key to good soil structure and humus in the soil. Your vegetable plants take nutrients out of the soil as they grow, so you need to replace those nutrients otherwise the soil becomes depleted. You will get a better yield of crops if they are grown in fertile and healthy soil. Adding compost over the years creates great soil that plants appreciate. The bottom line is, take good care of your soil and you'll enjoy more food to eat! Whenever you transplant a vegetable plant put a handful of compost in the hole to enrich the soil. In addition, put an 8 cm (3 in) layer of compost on top of the soil around the plant.

Compost Lovers

Some plants adore compost-rich soil. Tomatoes are a popular favourite; they are easy to grow and many people with no garden will find room for a container or bag of tomatoes. A tomato bought from a supermarket bears no resemblance to the fruit picked fresh from the plant, so it's no surprise that lots of people grow their own. If you grow your tomatoes in compost-enriched soil you'll be sure to get a bumper, flavourful crop. As mentioned above, put a generous handful of compost in the hole when you transplant your tomatoes and put a layer of compost on top of the soil around the plant, but not touching the delicate stem. If you're using a wormery, dilute some of the liquid fertilizer 10 times with water and use as a plant feed on your tomatoes. Alternatively, make comfrey tea as outlined in the chapter How to Compost (see page 86) and use that as a liquid feed. You can apply 1–2 cm (½ in) of compost monthly to the soil around tomatoes during the growing season.

Runner Beans and Squashes

Runner beans and squashes are crops that also benefit from compost, but in a different way. These plants like moisture-retentive soil in order to produce tender beans and bountiful crops. One of the easiest ways to achieve this is to trench compost. With trench composting, you dig a trench in the autumn where you plan to plant your beans or squash. Fill the trench with fruit and vegetable peelings and cover the trench with soil. The following spring plant your beans or squash directly in the trench. Refer to Compost Bins & Composting Systems for more details (see page 122).

Sulky Herbs

Some plants don't want your lovely compost. They prefer poor quality, well draining soil. Many herbs, for example, are used to growing in a Mediterranean climate on rocky slopes with poor soil. What they crave is not rich soil but maximum drainage. Thyme is a good example of a herb that prefers this condition. Lavender, basil and parsley, however, prefer richer soils. Refer to a book on herb gardening for specific details before using your compost on a herb that won't appreciate your efforts! Compost tea applied to the leaves, however, will result in a good crop of herbs that will taste great and attract all sorts of beneficial insects to your garden.

Compost Tea

Compost tea is not the sort of beverage that you can offer guests, but many of your plants and herbs will love it. In a similar way to making comfrey tea, compost tea is made by steeping the compost in water and using the resulting liquid in diluted form. Compost tea is used as a foliar feed and helps prevent diseases in your plants.

To Make Compost Tea

- Put a shovelful of compost into something like an **old pillowcase or sack** – a material where the water can seep in.
- Put this sack into a **large bucket** with 20 litres (5 gallons) of water.
- **Cover and leave** for up to a week.
- Take out the bag of compost and **squeeze** it to extract all the nutrients, just as you would if you were making a real cup of tea with a tea bag.
- **Dilute 10 times** with water then use the compost-infused 'tea' straight away on the leaves of your plants.
- Don't forget to make the most of your compost by turning the **wet compost** into your soil or adding it to a new compost heap!

> ## Tip
> Compost tea does not store well, so make as much as you need and use it straight away.

Recap

- **Healthy soil** needs around five per cent of organic matter to support healthy plant life.
- You need to **take care of the soil** rather than the plants.
- To improve **soil structure** mix a 10–15 cm (4–6 in) layer of finished compost into the soil.
- Compost makes **essential nutrients** available for plants to use.
- Compost can be used as **mulch**. To do this spread 8 cm (3 in) thick layers around plants.
- To use mulch as a **weed suppressant**, use thicker layers – around 10–15 cm (4–6 in).
- Refer to a good gardening book to discover which plants are **compost-lovers**.
- **Compost tea** makes a great plant food.

Seeds and Containers

Compost can give plants a great start to life when used as an ingredient in potting compost. You can use it in containers with great success and if you don't have a garden it is ideal for window boxes, hanging baskets and house plants. In this section you will learn how to make your own simple potting compost (potting medium or potting mix) and places for the 'non-gardener' to use compost.

Potting Compost

The compost you make at home is different to the product you buy, there's no doubt about it. If you have only ever used store-bought products then you'll need to get used to using home-made compost because it acts differently. Just using home-made compost would not be a suitable medium for growing seeds because it is often too acidic, but you can make your own potting mix quickly and easily. Store-bought compost has other components that enrich the nutrient and mineral content. You will need to add these yourself for raising seedlings as outlined in the recipes that follow. If this feels daunting, then continue to buy potting compost for seeds and use your own compost for other jobs in the garden.

Preparing the Compost

Before using your own home-made compost as an ingredient in potting mix, you'll need to prepare it. The first thing is to ensure it is fully cured. As mentioned previously, immature compost can damage or even kill small, vulnerable plants. Secondly, you will need to sieve your compost to make it finer. You'll probably have noticed that your compost is not as finely textured as a store-bought product. The tougher pieces left in the sieve can be thrown back into your next compost batch or dug into your soil.

Potting Compost Recipes

Here are two simple potting compost recipes. For the first one, combine together:

 one part home-made compost

 one part garden soil

 one part horticultural sand (do not use builders' sand)

Another recipe makes one small amendment and combines:

 one part home made compost

 one part garden soil

 one part leaf mould

Horticultural sand can be bought in garden centres and some DIY stores. Use either of these recipes just as you would use store-bought potting compost.

Container Gardening

Many people grow plants in pots. Pots can liven up a patio with colourful flowers. They are ideal for growing herbs next to the back door, which gives you access to your herbs for cooking and prevents some of the more tenacious ones from taking over your garden. People without gardens can grow tumbling tomatoes in hanging baskets or an assortment of salad leaves in a window box. The potting compost recipes are ideal for all containers such as plant pots, tubs and window boxes.

House Plants

Your house plants will love some of your compost too. Sprinkle a thin layer on top of their soil to provide nutrients. In an indoor environment, the air can become very dry, so the addition of compost to the soil of your house plants will help with water retention and stop your plants becoming too dry. You can also use your home-made potting mix when repotting; put a little of this into the bottom of the pot (after adding drainage materials such as gravel or broken crockery). Also remember to dilute and use liquid from your wormery or bokashi bin as a plant food throughout the growing season.

Tip

To see whether a houseplant needs repotting, check its roots; if they are coming out of the bottom of the pot, it's time to repot it.

Got a Brown Thumb?

For those with a brown thumb, here is a list of five house plants which are very difficult to kill:

 Cast Iron Plant (*Aspidistra elatior*)
 Dragon tree (*Dracaena marginata*)
 Mother-in-law's tongue (*Sansevieria*)
Spider Plant (*Chlorophytum comosum*)
ZZ plant (*Zamioculcas zamiifolia*)

Maybe a dose of your own compost sprinkled around the top of the soil will be all you need to turn your brown thumb green!

Recap

 Your compost can be used in **containers** and for **house plants**.

 Using neat, home-made compost for **seeds** is not a good idea; it needs to be mixed with other ingredients to make potting mix.

 Remember to use the **liquid** from your compost heap, wormery or bokashi bin for plant food.

 Sprinkle the top of the soil of your house plants with compost to retain **moisture**.

Elsewhere

Compost can be used virtually anywhere in your garden. In this section you'll learn about using it on your lawn, around trees and shrubs, and how to produce beautiful flowers. You will benefit from brighter, prolific blooms, healthy, strong trees, shrubs that are more resistant to disease and a lush, green lawn. At the end of the section we'll talk about recycling your spent compost too!

Lawn

Putting compost onto your lawn will help retain moisture, which is very important in hot, dry climates. Tiny bits of bark or twigs in the compost will help to hold the moisture, like hundreds of tiny sponges. When you apply compost to your lawn it keeps the moisture on the surface, which prevents excessive evaporation. This means you can go longer without watering and stressing the grass. By using compost, you will be adding nutrients to the grass for good growth and improving root strength.

Using Compost On the Lawn

If your lawn is healthy and only needs maintaining, then sprinkle a light dusting of compost over the grass and rake it over. Imagine that it is icing sugar on top of a cake – a very fine layer that you can hardly see. If your lawn is in need of some serious care, then you can apply compost up to 3 cm (1 in) thick over your lawn and leave it to be washed in by the rain. Apply compost in this way once a year, twice if your lawn is in poor health. It might look like a huge load of dirt on your grass for a while, but within a week or so it will have disappeared. All that will remain is a healthier-looking lawn.

HAve you Thought Of?

How much water you could save by mulching your soil?

Trees and Shrubs

Compost can be used around trees and shrubs in a number of ways. It can be added to the soil around your existing shrubs and trees to improve moisture retention, fertility and aeration of the soil around them. Late spring is a good time to do this. A 3 cm (1 in) thick layer of compost sprinkled around your trees and shrubs will gradually penetrate the soil and be highly beneficial for the health of your plants.

Planting New Trees and Shrubs

When planting new trees and shrubs, you can mix some of your compost with the soil from the hole you have dug. This will reduce the amount of watering you need to do and if you keep applying your compost to the soil around these plants you may eliminate the need for fertilizer as well. Remember to use your own compost, wormery or bokashi juice for a chemical-free fertilizer.

Mixing Compost and Soil for New Trees and Shrubs

For shrubs, mix three parts soil with one part compost. For trees mix four parts soil with one part compost. Use the soil from the hole you have dug – in some gardens you may need to sieve this first. After filling the hole, firm down the soil/compost mix slightly and water thoroughly.

Soil Amendment v. Mulch

Research was carried out at Washington State University to determine whether compost applied as a soil amendment or as mulch resulted in healthier trees. Over the course of the experiment it was noted that treatments with compost, compared to the control plants without compost, resulted in plants of higher quality. However, there was *no significant difference* in quality and growth increases between treatments with the compost incorporated into the soil and when the compost was left on the soil as a mulch.

Don't Sweat It!

From the evidence above, it would appear that if you've bought some new trees and shrubs, but your compost is not ready during planting, don't worry about it. Just use plenty of compost when it becomes available on the soil around the trees and shrubs and you will still see benefits!

Flowers

If you are starting a new flowerbed, you can dig compost into the soil up to 10 cm (4 in) down to give your plants a healthy start in life. If your flowers are already planted, then spread a thin layer of compost around the base of the plants, without going right up to the stem. Don't forget to keep the circle of life turning by adding your dead flowers to your compost heap.

Roses

Roses love rich soil and spreading your compost around the soil roses grow in will be very beneficial. You can also use compost tea as a foliar feed, which can help to prevent diseases and reduces the need for chemical fertilizers. Using compost as mulch reduces the need for watering as well. If you are planting new roses, dig the hole and mix two parts of the dug-out soil with one part of compost for refilling. You can protect your roses in winter by adding a thick mulch of compost around them through the cold season.

Rejuvenating Old Compost

Reuse your spent compost from containers and grow bags by adding it to your new compost pile in alternating layers with fresh ingredients. You can also use it as a top dressing on flower borders, put it in hanging baskets, or sprinkle it onto your lawn. Although there may not be many nutrients left, it will still improve the structure of the soil and increase moisture-retaining abilities.

Recap

- Compost can be used as a top dressing for **lawns**.
- Add compost to the soil around your **trees and shrubs** to improve their health.
- **Leave a gap** between compost and tender stems.
- When planting **shrubs** mix three parts soil with one part compost for filling the hole.
- Before planting **trees** mix four parts soil with one part compost for filling the hole.
- Most **flowers** will love the addition of compost to the soil they grow in.

Checklist

- Check which of your plants **love compost** and which ones don't in a good gardening book or website.

- Keep a little of your finished compost back for starting a **new batch**.

- How much compost have you made? You might need to **prioritize** where you use it, focusing on neglected soil first.

- Remember that you are **feeding the soil** not the plants. Healthy soil produces healthy plants.

- **Apply mulches** around established trees and shrubs in a 3–8 cm (1–3 in) layer.

- **Water plants** thoroughly before mulching, apply the mulch and then water again.

- Put a handful of compost into **transplanting holes** and around new plants.

- Before using up all your compost, make a batch of **compost tea** to use as a foliar feed.

- Where can you buy **horticultural sand**? Shop around for a good deal if you want to make your own potting compost.

- Sprinkle some compost **over your grass** for a green and lush lawn.

The Composting Year

The Composting Year

Every gardener works to the rhythms of nature; co-operation is far better than competition, as we have mentioned previously. Using compost at the right time and in the right place is no different. Throughout the year different needs will arise which are dependent, predominantly, on the weather.

Seasons in Different Hemispheres

In this section, the year has been divided into early, middle and late seasons. For the Northern hemisphere this equates roughly to early spring in March, mid spring in April, late spring in May and so on. For the Southern hemisphere this equates to early spring in September, mid spring in October and late spring in November etc. See below:

Season	Northern Hemisphere	Southern Hemisphere
Early Spring	March	September
Mid Spring	April	October
Late Spring	May	November
Early Summer	June	December
Mid Summer	July	January
Late Summer	August	February
Early Autumn	September	March
Mid Autumn	October	April
Late Autumn	November	May
Early Winter	December	June
Mid Winter	January	July
Late Winter	February	August

Spring

Spring is when the gardener's year gets under way. The days are lengthening and the sun is stronger. The budding of new life is evident and the push towards regrowth gathers momentum.

Compost Heap and Mulching During Spring

During the spring, your compost heap will 'wake up' with the increase in daily temperatures. Digging a layer of compost into the soil prior to planting will give your seeds and plants a good start to life. During spring the grass gets its first cut of the year; add the clippings to your compost heap as a nitrogen-rich green with other browns for balance. Once your comfrey plants start to grow, cut and add the leaves to your compost heap. Alternatively gather spring nettles. Both of these are good activators to stimulate the decomposition process. Mulching during the spring helps to keep the ground warm for plants and keeps weeds at bay.

Early Spring

During early spring plants resume growth, the lawn begins to grow and sowing and planting can take place. There can be wide variations in day-to-day weather conditions during early spring, which means that you need to be flexible with your plans. Sometimes early spring brings long days of warm sunshine; in other climates it rains relentlessly and temperatures remain low with night frosts. In some climates during early spring the ground is still covered in a thick blanket of snow and you'll have to wait before you can do much outdoors.

A False Sense of Security

Don't fall into the trap of thinking a few days of warm temperatures means that spring has finally arrived! The weather can change in an instant, and if you've been busy sowing seeds and planting out, all your hard work could be lost. Make the most of warm, dry days, but it is safer to delay sowing or planting rather than be caught out by a subsequent cold spell.

Containers and House Plants

For those with a small garden, you can still grow vegetables and enjoy some self-sufficiency. Try salad onions, lettuce and radishes in a sheltered window box or other container. Adding some compost to the mix will provide moisture-retaining soil that your plants will love. If there are signs of new growth on your house plants, then you can apply some liquid feed from your bokashi bin or wormery. Take off any dead leaves from your house plants and add them to your compost heap. This is a good time to repot plants. Choose a pot one or two sizes larger than the one your plant is already in, add some drainage materials in the bottom, such as gravel, and place some home-made potting mix in the bottom. See the chapter Using Compost for recipes (see page 173). Repot the plant, water and apply a fine layer of compost over the surface of the soil.

Lawns

If you have bare patches on your established lawn, you can re-seed now. A sprinkling of compost before you sow the seed will be beneficial and establish healthy, strong roots. While you are doing this, aerate the rest of your lawn to improve drainage and apply some of your home-made fertilizer, such as juice from a bokashi bin or wormery. Dilute wormery juice 10 times with water and bokashi juice 100 times with water before use. When your grass reaches 6–8 cm (2.5–3 in) it will need the first cut of the season. If you are planning on planting a new lawn then dig compost into the ground and rake the surface of the soil. Then spread your chosen seed mixture and rake the seed in. When you do your first cut, remember to put your grass clippings into the compost bin or use as mulch on other areas of your garden.

Roses and Flowers

This is the latest time in the year to plant roses. Remember that roses love rich soil, so fill the hole you are putting them into with a 50/50 mix of garden soil and compost. After planting, water the rose in, and sprinkle a generous layer of compost around them, without touching the stem. Take care of established roses by cutting back diseased wood and do any pruning that may be required. Some annual flower seeds can be sown now. Use your home-made potting mix to plant them in. Flowers such as begonias, calendulas, cornflower, dahlia, petunia, lobelia and love-in-the-mist will bring colour to your garden later in the year. Some of the early spring bulb flowers will die off now, so deadhead them and add to the compost bin.

Trees, Hedges and Shrubs

Any young trees and shrubs will love a dressing of compost on the soil around them to retain moisture. Don't push it right up against the stem or trunk, but apply generously in a layer around the plants. Weed underneath hedges so that the weeds do not compete for light and food and put the weeds on the compost heap. If you are planting a new hedge this year, put lots of compost in the bottom of the hole before planting.

Vegetables, Fruit and Herbs

You can plant tomato seeds in pots now – tomatoes love compost, so make your own potting mix, selecting one of the recipes from the chapter Using Compost (see page 173) and use it for your seeds. If the ground has warmed up enough to dig, this is the traditional time to plant out early potatoes. While you dig the trench for your potatoes, add some compost and mix it in. Potato trenches are usually 30 cm (1 ft) deep and you can add 6–8 cm (2–3 in) of compost to the bottom of the trench. You can sow other vegetables at this time of year too, such as Brussels sprouts, parsnips, summer cabbages, spinach and leeks, in your potting mix. Prepare a seed bed for herbs as soon as it is warm enough. Some herbs, as previously mentioned, do not like rich soils; they prefer well-drained, poor soils. However, parsley and chives can be planted with some home-made potting mix as they prefer a richer soil.

Weeds and Ponds

Weed plant beds and add the weeds to your compost heap. You can also use some of your old compost as mulch to improve the soil and act as a weed suppressant. If you are digging over a bed to pull out weeds, then add compost as you go, especially if it is a new or neglected bed. This will improve the soil structure. If you have a pond then do some maintenance, which should include removing any weed mass from the water. Too many weeds, such as algae, can deprive the water of oxygen and turn the water green. Pondweed is high in nitrogen and is a good activator for the compost heap.

Mid Spring

Mid spring can bring warmer temperatures, but lots of rain! In some areas you can still find frost and cold daytime temperatures; the weather is still quite variable. You should be enjoying beautiful displays of bulbs and you'll need to mow the grass more regularly in many areas.

If you have the space, a couple of water butts in your garden will enable you to gather valuable rainwater for use later in the year. Traditionally, mid spring is the time of year when most sowing and planting out takes place.

Containers and House Plants

If the weather was not warm enough during early spring, you can now plant salad leaves and radishes in a window box or container. Mix in some of your compost and you'll enjoy a feast later in the year. If you have container-grown trees and shrubs, you can carefully remove the top 5 cm (2 in) of soil and replace it with fresh compost. Vegetables such as broad (fava) beans, carrots and chard can now be sown in containers. If your house plants have started to grow, feed them with home-made fertilizer from your wormery or bokashi bin.

Lawns

You might find that you need to mow your grass once or twice a week now. Use the cuttings as mulch, add to your compost bin or leave on the grass to work their way in. If your lawn needs some maintenance then add a fine sprinkling of your home-made compost on top of the lawn after cutting. Use about 1 cm ($1/8$–$1/4$ in) and leave it to work into the ground to improve the health of the grass roots. If you were unable to sow grass seed last month due to poor weather conditions, you should be able to sow them now. Use a layer of compost under the seed for a good start to life.

Have you Thought Of?

Installing some water butts in your garden will make the most of rainfall and reduce your need for tap water.

Roses and Other Flowers

Keep applying some of your home-made fertilizers to roses and either use your grass cuttings
or compost as a thick mulch around them. Up to a 3 cm (1 in) thick layer of compost or 2 cm
($^1/_2$ in) grass cuttings is fine. Remember not to mulch too close to the rose stems. You should be
enjoying some spring bulbs; deadhead them regularly and add the spent leaves to your compost
heap. Add mulch to your flower borders – either your own compost or grass clippings.

Trees and Shrubs

Any new trees or shrubs like to have moist and cool roots. Using grass clippings or compost as mulch is the perfect solution. This will also help suppress weeds. When you plant them, add some well rotted compost or leaf mould to the bottom of the hole. A 50/50 mix of the original soil and compost is ideal. Early flowering shrubs that have finished flowering can be pruned. Shred the old woody prunings and keep them to add to your compost pile throughout the year.

Vegetables, Fruit and Herbs

Potatoes can be planted out during mid spring. Line the trench with compost for a bumper yield (and some say a better-tasting crop!). Peas, carrots, beetroot, cabbages and cauliflowers can be planted too. Check the seed packets or a gardening book to find out what sort of soil they like. Plant more parsley now for a continual crop later in the year. Parsley can take nine weeks to germinate, so be patient! You can plant basil too – both of these herbs like richer soils, so make your own potting mix and use it.

Weeds and Ponds

Continue pulling weeds, leave them to dry for a few days and then add them to the compost heap. As the weather heats up the amount of weeds growing will increase; so keeping on top of them now is important. If you let them mature and go to seed, it will make your weeding job much more difficult. The same goes for ponds; keep removing blankets of thick weed and add them to the compost heap.

Late Spring

Late spring can bring warm, dry days. However, there can sometimes be a late frost that catches gardeners out! If you haven't done so already, install a couple of water butts so that you have water throughout the drier seasons. During this busy season of sowing, planting and drier days, it's imperative that you have enough water to sustain your plants. Late spring can feel like an overwhelming time in the garden; there is a lot to do and everything is growing so quickly! Keep short accounts; half an hour here and there to keep on top of things.

Containers and House Plants

Hanging baskets can be planted now. Line the basket with soaked coir and add some of your home-made potting mix before adding your chosen plants. If you are growing salad leaves, then continue planting to enjoy a continual crop. You can plant French beans, cucumbers, courgettes (zucchini) and peas in containers too. Refer to a container-planting book for further information about what can be planted when. If you've been growing winter bedding plants and they have come to an end, add the contents to your compost bin and decide on what you might like to plant next to bring interest and colour to your pots. If they need rich soil then make sure you have enough of your home-made compost to add to the soil. Finish repotting any house plants now and continue to feed with your own fertilizer. Either wormery juice diluted 10 times with water or bokashi juice diluted 100 times is ideal.

Lawns

As your lawn will be growing so rapidly, you might need to cut the grass twice a week. Mow your lawn regularly and use the grass clippings as mulch around plants or dry them and add them to your compost heap with some balancing browns. From time to time, leave the clippings on the lawn to return valuable nitrogen to the grass. This can be particularly helpful if the weather is dry as the clippings act as mulch too; protecting the grass from heat. You can still sow grass seed or lay turf if you have not done so already. Put down a fine layer of your compost before sowing seed.

Roses and Flowers

You can still make sowings of some hardy or half-hardy annuals and hardy perennials. For flowers that like rich, fertile soil mix in some of your compost with the soil before sowing. Continue to deadhead the flowers from spring bulbs and add these to the compost heap. Sweet pea plants can be mulched to conserve moisture and restrict weed growth.

Trees, Shrubs and Hedges

Some hedges will need pruning between now and September to retain their shape. Shred the prunings finely and keep them as a valuable brown for your compost heap. As the days warm up, it's even more important to retain as much moisture as you can in your garden. Mulching is the perfect way to ensure this. Use a thick layer of compost or keep grass clippings for this job.

Vegetables, Fruit and Herbs

You can now prepare the site for the squash family including marrows, courgettes (zucchini) and pumpkins. These plants like rich soil so dig a hole and fill the bottom with compost before refilling with soil. You can then put two or three seeds in each hole if the weather is warm enough and leave the strongest to grow for later in the year. Runner beans can be planted in the same way. If you have not trench composted during the autumn, then dig a trench and fill the bottom with compost before topping up with soil and planting your beans. You can continue to plant parsley and basil seeds in pots with your own potting mix. In addition, you can divide mint and put some in a pot with potting compost. Mint will grow in virtually any soil, but prefers something a bit richer.

Have You Thought Of?

Doing a small amount of gardening every day can save you time in the long run and prevent tenacious weeds getting established.

Weeds and Ponds

As the sunlight increases, so can algae in a pond. Remove this from time to time with a stick and add it to the compost heap with some browns such as shredded cardboard or paper. You might be getting a lot of weeds growing in your garden now. Try and go outside daily, even for just ten minutes, and pull them out while they are young. Dry them in the sun and add to your compost heap. Try weeding on dry days to prevent the weeds recovering. Did you know that you can grow watercress in a pond? Why not have a go!

Summer

During summer, temperatures often soar and there are plenty of hot, sunny days to enjoy. The most important thing during this time is to ensure your plants and lawn get enough water. If you've installed water butts, you'll be able to take advantage of any rainfall and use it during long, dry spells. Plants prefer rainwater and you will see a marked difference when using rainwater compared to tap water.

Compost Heap and Mulching During Summer

Mulching throughout the summer protects the soil from relentless heat and helps to reduce water evaporation. This is better for both your plants and for the environment, because you can consume less water in the garden. With the higher temperatures your compost heap will really take off. Ensure a good mix of greens and browns and keep checking for that wrung-out sponge consistency. If your compost heap feels dry then it won't cook properly; you'll need to add some water and mix it in.

Early Summer

Early summer can bring long, sunny days, but temperatures can still fall at night. It's usually dry so it's important to retain moisture around your garden and keep weeds in check – they grow almost overnight with the high sun! Throughout the summer you'll want to pay attention to mulching around moisture-loving plants to retain water in the soil and protect the soil from extremes of temperature.

Time For a Hot Heap?

If you are considering setting up a hot (active) compost heap, then early summer is a great time to begin. Refer back to the chapter How to Compost for instructions on hot composting (see page 68). Early summer provides the gardener with lots of green ingredients and, if you've been saving browns, it should not be difficult to fill a hot heap. Remember to add some comfrey or nettle leaves and you'll be using your compost by the autumn.

Containers

Continue successional sowing of salad leaves in a container with a mix of your home-made compost and soil. Rocket (arugula) is a delicious salad leaf that can be planted in containers. Hanging baskets can add colour to your garden and are ideal for those with small or no gardens. Make up some potting mix following one of the recipes in the chapter Using Compost (see page 173). You can even grow certain tumbling varieties of tomatoes in hanging baskets. These are ideal for people without gardens who wish to grow some of their own food. For large potted plants that haven't been repotted, give them some of your plant food; wormery or bokashi juice is ideal. If you don't have any, then compost tea is also good. Place mulch around containers with leaf mould, grass clippings or a thick layer of compost.

Lawns

You will have lots of grass clippings throughout the summer. Put them to great use by adding to the compost heap with browns or using as mulch around water-loving plants. Alternatively, if you are in a dry climate, leaving the clippings on your grass will help retain moisture. This can be particularly helpful during times of drought. In addition, regularly spiking the lawn to allow any rain or water to sink down will make a big difference to the quality of your grass during dry times.

Roses and Flowers

Early summer is a wonderful time of year to enjoy flowers in your garden. Keep flowerbeds and pots mulched to retain moisture. If you are new to gardening then geraniums are ideal flowers; they are easy to take care of and will survive a bit of neglect. Some species are unfussy when it comes to weather conditions – shade or sun, they will provide you with an array of colour.

Trees, Shrubs and Hedges

Plants in your garden will start to grow rapidly. Keep hedges trimmed to prevent them becoming straggly and store any shredded cuttings to add to your compost heap. Shrubs with flowers will need to be deadheaded and the flowers can be added to your compost heap. Continue to mulch around moisture-loving plants with compost or grass clippings.

Vegetables, Fruit and Herbs

Tomato plants will be hungry, so use some of the home-made fertilizer from your wormery or bokashi to feed them. You can still plant marrows in compost-rich soil and there are plenty of other crops that can be sown too. Planting in succession means that you can enjoy a longer harvesting season. Try French or runner beans, peas, beetroot, swedes (rutabaga), cauliflower, cucumber or sweetcorn. Refer to a gardening book to find out which ones will benefit from some of your compost. Chives can be sown at this time of year – they need high temperatures to germinate and they love rich, moist soil. Make your own potting mix to provide the ideal soil.

Weeds and Ponds

This is usually the worst time of year for weeds! Try and get out in your garden every day, even if it's just for ten minutes to keep on top of the weeding. You can dry weeds in the sun until they shrivel and then add them to your compost heap. It is better to hoe off weeds as small seedlings than let them mature. More sun can lead to rapid algae growth in ponds. Keep pulling the blankets of weeds out, check for anything living in the weeds, such as tiny fish or snails, remove them and then add the weed to your compost heap.

Mid summer

Hopefully this is the hottest time of year. Attention must be given to ensuring that there is enough water in the garden – mulching is an ideal way of supporting this. Depending on your climate, there may be a lot of humidity during mid summer or heavy thunderstorms to deal with. Hoeing also helps to retain moisture – it breaks up the top layer of the soil, which helps to keep water in the soil rather than evaporating.

Containers and House Plants

Containers require a lot of water to retain healthy moisture levels. Adding a layer of compost to the top of containers can help slow evaporation rates. Remember to water pots regularly to prevent any casualties. It is better to give pots a good soak, less frequently, than to adopt a little-and-often watering routine. If you do the latter, plants will put down shallow roots and become more susceptible to disease. If you make them put down deep roots to find water, they will be stronger and healthier. Be aware that even after rain, many containers and hanging baskets will not be wet enough, so check the moisture levels of the soil. A lot of the time rain just bounces off the leaves and doesn't reach the compost at all.

Lawns

If you live in an area that is prone to droughts, then it is better to keep the grass a bit longer to retain moisture; aim for about 3 cm (1 in). When cutting the lawn, keep the grass clippings for your compost bin or leave in situ to help keep moisture in the grass. From time to time mow your grass without the grass box on and allow the clippings to rot down into your lawn. This will happen very quickly during the hot weather and will feed your grass with nitrogen.

Roses and Flowers

Once roses lose their initial first flush of blooms, you can use some home-made fertilizer on them – either bokashi or worm juice, diluted with water or compost tea, will be well received. Deadhead other flowers as and when and add them to your compost pile, and cut back anything that is growing rampantly and threatening to take over the flower garden.

Trees, Shrubs and Hedges

Continue to trim back hedges and use the prunings as a valuable brown for your compost heap. If you do not have enough greens to balance the amount of hedge trimmings you have, then shred them up and store them somewhere dry until you need them. Trees and shrubs that were planted earlier in the year will require a lot of water to keep them healthy. Remember to mulch around plants to help retain moisture.

Vegetables, Fruit and Herbs

Pick up any fruit that has dropped and prune heavy croppers. Any inedible fruit can be added to your compost heap. Cover fruit with a layer of grass clippings or shredded paper to prevent fruit flies and wasps. Shallots and onions can be lifted and dried. The papery outside skins and leaves can be added to the compost heap. You can still plant parsley seeds in the ground. Parsley likes a richer soil than some herbs, so mix in a handful of compost while sowing. Mid summer is a time for drying herbs and lavender. Cut back the lavender stems you need and add any woody bits to the compost bin. You should be enjoying a good crop of all sorts of vegetables now!

Weeds and Ponds

Continue to remove any weeds such as blanket weed and algae from the pond. You can also prune plants in the pond – all of these can be added to your compost heap as a valuable nitrogen-rich ingredient. Leave any pondweeds by the side of your pond for a couple of days after gathering so that any tiny creatures caught up in the plants can get back into the water. You'll need to keep on top of garden weeds too. Hoe around plants, even if you can't see weeds because you'll help to break up the top layer of soil and there will be bound to be some tiny weed seedlings that you haven't seen. Gather up any large weeds, leave them to dry in the sun and add to your compost heap.

Late Summer

Depending on your climate, you'll either be enjoying long, hot, hazy days of sunshine, enduring thunderstorms or be feeling a touch of autumn in the air. You may still need to do a lot of watering and mulching to keep things moist, or you may be getting night dew, which makes your task easier. Generally, late summer means you can relax more in the garden; growth isn't so virulent and you can enjoy all your hard work.

Compost During Late Summer

Late summer is another good time to start a compost heap – a cold (passive) heap can be set up now. You can fill it between late summer and late autumn (once all the pruning is over), leave it over winter and use it in spring. Keep adding raw ingredients throughout the summer and autumn and then perhaps insulate the heap to keep it cooking throughout the winter – see the chapter How to Compost (page 81) for more information. If you have particularly harsh winters, it might be best to start to compost in early spring.

Containers and House Plants

Continue to water and mulch containers as necessary. Continue to feed with one of your home-made fertilizers – either wormery or bokashi juice or compost tea. Remember to water containers and hanging baskets even after rainfall. It is unusual for the rain to find its way down into the compost; instead it bounces off the leaves. You can still sow salad crops such as lettuce, rocket (arugula) and mizuna in containers or window boxes. If your summer is particularly hot and dry, you may have to move your containers to a shadier spot, to prevent them drying out too much.

Lawns

It can be tempting to water lawns in the height of summer, especially if they develop brown patches, but in all but the harshest of climates, this really is a waste of water. As soon as the rain comes, grass will recover. Save water for plants that will die without it. Keeping the grass cut, but not too short, and letting the grass clippings rot back into the lawn is a good way to ensure a healthy, green lawn throughout the season. A mulching mower is a great investment if you have a lot of lawn and you want to keep it looking good. These machines shred the clippings incredibly finely and spread them over the lawn, which looks much tidier and keeps the lawn healthy. It does mean, however, that you don't have any grass clippings to add to your compost or use on other areas of your garden. If your lawn is looking tired you can sprinkle and rake a layer of compost over the grass as a top dressing.

Roses and Flowers

Deadheading is an important task. This can encourage new flowering later on and helps remove a potential source of disease from your flowers. Add any spent blooms to the compost heap. Annuals will stop producing flowers altogether if allowed to set seed, so spend some time walking around your garden daily, removing dead flowers and having a tidy up. Keep mulching around your flowerbeds. If you have repeat-flowering

roses, it is particularly important to remove fading blooms so that you can enjoy the second flush.

Trees, Shrubs and Hedges

Continue to keep hedges in shape by trimming them. Store shredded hedge trimmings to use as a brown in your compost heap. Some shrubs will produce new flowering shoots if they are deadheaded. When you take a stroll around your garden in the evening, look at your shrubs and see if there are any shoots to remove. Add these to your compost heap. Keep shrubs, trees and hedges well mulched, especially if you live in a very hot, dry climate.

Vegetables, Fruit and Herbs

Late summer is harvest time! You can enjoy all your hard work by eating some of your home-grown produce. This is a very rewarding and satisfying time of year. It's time to start thinking ahead about herbs; in a couple of months there will be very few fresh herbs in the garden. Some, such as rosemary, thyme, sage and bay will last all year long, but others, such as basil and mint, will die back. You can pot up some herbs to grow indoors throughout the winter months. Chives, mint and parsley can be brought indoors and put in a pot with gritty compost. To do this: fill the pot you want to use with your regular potting mix, tip it out into a bowl, and fill the same pot one quarter full with coarse horticultural sand. Mix the sand and potting mix together and use this as your gritty potting compost. Continue to mulch around the herbs in your garden.

Weeds and Ponds

The good news is that weed growth should have slowed down considerably by now, but keep that hoe of yours busy! Keep a daily or twice-weekly eye on things and hoe off and remove any weeds as they appear. Let them dry in the sun and add them to your compost heap. Continue to remove blanket weed and algae from your pond. Leave them by the side of the pond for a couple of days to allow tiny creatures to get back into the water, and then add the weeds to your compost heap.

Autumn

Autumn is the traditional time to begin a compost heap, ready for use in the spring. The other important task during autumn is gathering leaves to make leaf mould. In addition, you will be harvesting crops if you are growing food. It's a wonderful time of year when you can reflect on what has and has not worked and make plans for next year's garden.

Compost Heap and Mulching During Autumn

During autumn, mulching keeps the ground warm. It is also a popular time to add compost to the surface of the soil. Adding to the surface means that the worms and the rain do all the digging for you over the next few months! Some gardeners begin their compost heaps in autumn whilst others start them in spring; do whichever is right for you.

Early Autumn

The weather can be changeable as autumn arrives. Days can still be warm, but night temperatures fall and you might wake up to dew on the ground. In some climates, you might have to protect your compost heap against high winds; especially if it is an open pile.

Containers and House Plants

As blooms and plants die in containers, they can be taken out and added to the compost pile. Add the spent compost to the heap as well and start with fresh soil. If you want spring-flowering bulbs then now is the time to plant them. Add some home-made potting mix to your container, plant the bulbs and cover with compost, leaving the tops of the bulbs poking through the soil. Most house plants' growth will now slow down, so you can stop feeding them. Remove any dead leaves or flowers and add them to the compost heap. Have a go at growing

rocket (arugula) in a container. If you get a relatively mild season, you might be enjoying it right through to winter. Lamb's lettuce is a hardy winter salad that can be grown in your own potting mix and enjoyed throughout the winter.

Lawns

If you want to lay turf, early autumn is a great time to do this. Prepare the soil beforehand by adding a layer of compost. If you only have a few bare patches on your lawn, then put down a handful of compost and sprinkle grass seed into the spaces. This is a good time to sprinkle a layer of compost on a well-maintained lawn and rake it over.

Roses and Flowers

You can plant spring-flowering bulbs now. Make a hole where you want the bulb to go, put some compost in the bottom of the hole and fill over with fine soil. Continue to deadhead and tidy up your flower borders. Add the spent plants to your compost heap and mulch around flowers to keep the soil warm as temperatures drop.

Trees, Shrubs and Hedges

Early autumn is a great time to plant shrubs, hedges and trees. The ground will be moist, but still warm. The addition of some home-made compost to each planting hole will benefit your chosen plants. A final cut to hedges can be given. Store the shredded cuttings to use in the compost heap. Do a final weed around the bottom of your hedges and add the weeds to your compost heap. If leaves are beginning to fall, gather them up to make your own leaf mould.

Vegetables and Fruit

Harvest fruits for storage such as apples and pears. As you pick the fruit, damaged ones can be chopped up and added to the compost heap. Whilst you are picking the fruit, you can also prune the trees. Woody branches can be shredded and stored for adding to the compost heap later. Take out any remaining vegetable plant parts from the soil, such as cabbage stumps, chop them up and add them to the pile. Gather crops like tomatoes and courgettes before the frosts arrive otherwise they will end up on the compost heap too! You can continue to plant small pots of herbs such as chives, mint and parsley for indoor use during the winter. Refer back to the 'Late Summer' section to find out how to use your own gritty potting mix (see page 203).

> **Tip**
>
> Put a net over your pond to catch fallen leaves; this will make it easy to gather them up and add to your leaf mould pile.

Weeds and Ponds

Autumn can be a busy time in the gardening year with fruits and vegetables to harvest and general tidying-up to do. Keep going around your garden and removing weeds. These can be dried and added to the compost heap. Blanket weed growth in the pond should be slowing down now, but keep an eye on things and make sure your pond does not become choked up.

Mid Autumn

Mid autumn can be a beautiful time of year with sunny days and cool nights. In some areas this time of year brings a lot of rain, which means working the ground can be challenging. In an ideal situation, mid autumn will involve digging over the soil, adding compost and mulching, in preparation for springtime planting. By mid autumn, your compost bin might be getting very full, so if you have some comfrey plants, take a few leaves off, add them to the pile, give everything a mix around and leave. If you have room, this might be the time to begin another heap and leave the original pile to cook. Keep your compost heap covered now to keep the warmth in and rain out.

Containers and House Plants

Continue to empty containers of spent plants and place these in your compost heap. Depending on your climate, you may need to protect trees and shrubs in containers from the cold. You can use a thick layer of compost, straw or mulch for this.

Lawns

If the soil is still warm, you can lay turf. The moisture in the soil during autumn can make this a good time to lay a healthy lawn with strong roots. And it means the grass has a chance to establish before winter arrives. Sprinkle a layer of compost on the soil before laying the turf. Any bare patches can be sown with grass seed; sprinkle a fine layer of compost on the prepared area and sow the seed on top.

Roses and Flowers

You can finish planting spring-flowering bulbs during mid autumn. Bulbs prefer loose, well-draining, rich soil, so use your compost in the planting holes and around the bulbs as mulch.

Mulching helps protect against winter extremes of temperature so that you can enjoy a beautiful springtime show of colour. If you are planning on planting new roses, then now is the time to prepare the bed; dig well, incorporating leaf mould or compost. Prepare any flowerbeds for the following spring too. You can make this task easier by simply spreading a thick layer of compost on top of the soil as mulch and allowing the worms and rain to take it down into the soil throughout the winter.

Trees, Shrubs and Hedges

Continue to plant shrubs, hedges and trees during mid autumn and mix some home-made compost into each planting hole. If you didn't do your final hedge trimming at the beginning of the season, finish off now, shred the woody pieces and use them as a brown in your compost heap. Continue to rake and gather leaves and add them to your leaf mould pile. Depending on your climate, you may still need to be regularly watering and mulching plants to retain moisture. Those in damper climates can ease off, but mulching is still important to reduce evaporation and to help keep the soil warm.

Vegetables, Fruit and Herbs

Dig over the vegetable bed, incorporating some compost, and leave the frost to break up the soil. If your soil is in good condition, the best way to do this is to adopt the 'no dig' method of gardening. Simply layer compost thickly on the ground and leave it; over the next few months, the worms and rain will take the compost into the soil. If you have grown any nitrogen-rich plants, such as peas and beans, leave the roots in the ground to enrich the soil but you can add the leaves to the compost straight away. Your herb bed will be dying back now; fork over any bare soil and mulch with leaf mould.

Weeds and Ponds

Thin out oxygenating plants and dead leaves to reduce decaying vegetation on the bottom of the pond. These can be added to your compost heap. Go around your garden and clear away any weeds. Leave them for a few days to dry out before adding them to the compost heap.

Late Autumn

In between the cold, harsh days there is still plenty to do in the garden, like clearing things up before winter arrives and finishing off any planting. Some plants will already be dormant, others will still be showing signs of life. There may be frosts in some areas, snow in others, but many will still enjoy the odd warm, sunny day. Take advantage of the good weather to get things tidied up.

Containers and House Plants

If you live in a colder climate, keep terracotta containers protected from frost. You might even need to move them to a warmer spot if you live in a very cold region. Apply mulch around the soil to keep it warm. You can grow lamb's lettuce all through the season; why not plant a successional crop to enjoy this lovely salad all year around?

Lawns

Rake up any leaves that fall onto your grass. They can smother the grass, weaken and even kill it. Use the leaves to make leaf mould (see page 142). Take out any weeds and add them to your compost heap. If the ground is still dry, you can continue cutting the grass until it stops growing for the season. This will vary greatly depending on where you live.

Roses and Flowers

As long as the ground is not hard from frost, you can plant roses. Dig out the hole, mix in some compost and plant firmly. If your ground is not too sticky or wet, you can dig over any areas that might be used for flowers next year; work in some compost as you dig. Try not to leave any bare earth – cover it with leaf mould as mulch as this helps to keep the soil warm, protect it from extremes of temperature and prevent weed seeds taking hold. Your job will be easier during spring if you have stopped weeds growing now by mulching.

Trees, Shrubs and Hedges

Continue to gather fallen leaves for your leaf mould pile. You might remember from the chapter Other Types of Composting (see page 142) that oak and beech leaves take a particularly long time to rot down. If you have plants that need a 'winter coat' to help them through the cold weather, then you can use fallen oak and beech leaves as mulch. Apply a thick layer around your plants and cover with sticks to stop them blowing around. Any new evergreens planted earlier in the year might still need watering until the ground freezes. Evergreens require more water than deciduous plants because they continue to transpire through their leaves.

Vegetables, Fruit and Herbs

Late autumn is an important time in the garden. While things are not growing rapidly, you'll have time to do some garden maintenance and get things tidy. Keep on top of weeds by mulching well and not leaving any soil exposed. Adding mulches such as leaf mould protects the soil from temperature extremes and reduces weed growth. If you do some work now by suppressing weeds, you'll be ready to enjoy your garden in the spring, rather than having to play catch-up.

Weeds and Ponds

If you haven't done so already, cut back overgrown pond plants and remove any excess weeds. Leave the plants for a couple of days next to the pond to allow creatures to find their way back to the water. Pondweeds and plants can be added to the compost heap. Covering any bare ground in your garden with mulch is a great way to reduce weed growth. Remove any weeds from your garden, add them to the compost heap, then cover the bare soil with a protective mulch such as leaf mould or a thick layer of compost.

Winter

During the winter, the ground and some plants need protecting from extreme temperatures. Depending on your climate you might have several feet of snow, cold frosts or a lot of rain. Other climates have warmer winters where keeping things warm is not a problem.

Compost Heap and Mulching During Winter

Mulching during the winter protects the ground from extremes of temperature. During the winter the mulch will be taken down into the ground where it will condition your soil. The compost heap will probably slow down during this season as temperatures drop. Insulate your heap if possible with straw or other suitable material. As long as there is room, you can keep adding to the pile. You'll be amazed that even in sub-zero temperatures it still rots down a little. A compost heap can come to a complete halt in extreme weather but, if there is room, keep adding to it and once spring arrives your compost heap will begin working again. It is a good idea to turn the heap every couple of weeks during winter; an aerating tool or stick is ideal for this. If you have an outdoor worm bin, you may need to insulate it or move it indoors. Rainfall can wash nutrients from the soil, so try to cover exposed areas with leaf mould or fresh autumn leaves.

Early Winter

Early winter is another clearing and tidying time if weather conditions are favourable. You can continue to tidy, prune and gather up leaves. Often there is little sunshine at the beginning of winter and it gets colder. It is difficult to garden between the rain and frosts, but doing a little bit every day will keep things in order.

Containers

Terracotta planters can suffer during the winter; surround them with bubble wrap, hessian or some other insulating material to protect vulnerable plants from frost damage and keep your pots in one piece! Keep a layer of thick mulch on top of the soil to protect from extremes of temperature.

Tip

If you have a lot of oak or beech leaves, which take a long time to decompose, gather them up and use as ground cover during the winter.

Lawns

If you are planning on sowing grass seed in the spring, then now is the time to prepare the seedbed. Dig over the area and incorporate some compost, then leave until the spring when you can rake an even surface. Make sure you have gathered up and removed leaves from your lawn; add these to your leaf mould pile.

Roses and Flowers

Try to finish digging over new beds and borders for next year's flowers before the ground gets too hard. Incorporate compost as you are digging. Alternatively, leave a thick layer of compost on the surface and allow the worms and rain to do the work throughout the winter.

Trees, Shrubs and Hedges

Fruit trees can be pruned and you can continue to gather fallen leaves to add to your leaf mould pile. If the weather is dry, you can continue to plant green shrubs, conifers and hedging. Prepare the soil well and be generous with the compost!

Tip

It can be useful to have a large calendar or wall planner specifically for your 'gardening year'.

Vegetables, Fruit and Herbs

If you're planning to grow runner beans the following year then dig a trench and do some trench composting as outlined in Compost Bins & Composting Systems (see page 122). If you live in a very cold climate, some herbs, such as marjoram and rosemary, will benefit from a protective layer of leaf mould or straw around the soil to keep them warm.

Mid Winter

Mid winter can be the coldest month of the year. In some areas there will be several feet of snow, in others driving gales and many will have night temperatures below freezing for weeks on end. There is little to do in the garden, so it's a great time to read gardening books and browse through seed catalogues for inspiration. Keep adding your kitchen scraps to your compost heap, along with some shredded cardboard or paper. As the days gradually warm, towards the end of winter, your compost heap will start to work more quickly again. You can use this time to mix up batches of potting mix, as outlined in the chapter Using Compost (see page 173), ready for the spring. Ensure that your compost is covered to keep the rain out and the heat in.

Something Different

As you won't be spending so much time in the garden during mid winter, why not try making your own biodegradable plant pots for sowing time? You can use the cardboard inners from toilet rolls or newspaper and a paper potter. Paper potters are available online and from garden stores. To use a paper potter, you cut a newspaper into long strips, roll them around the paper potter and fold excess paper over to make the bottom of the pot. You then mould the pot into shape. Each pot takes a few seconds to make. You can plant seeds in them, water them without them disintegrating and then plant the whole thing in the ground. Once in the ground, they will gradually biodegrade. To make seedling pots from toilet roll inners, simply make four slits a quarter of the way up each tube and fold them in like the bottom of a cardboard box.

Late Winter

During late winter we catch glimpses of spring. Snowdrops and other bulbs show signs of life and warmer spells give you the chance to begin planting. Have a wander around your garden and clear up any old plants, twigs and leaves and add them to your compost heap.

Containers and House Plants

Some mini vegetables, such as carrots, salad onions and spinach, can be planted in well-protected containers. Mix in some of your compost with the soil and follow a gardening book to check the best time for sowing different crops. Container grown herbs will appreciate a bit of TLC now. Carefully remove the top 5–10 cm (2–4 in) of soil and replace with fresh compost or worm compost mixed with leaf mould. Any pots or plants at risk

from frost damage can be moved or insulated with bubble wrap or old hessian sacks. A layer of mulch will help too.

Lawns

Little needs doing to lawns at this time of year. Keep raking up leaves for your leaf mould pile. Aerating, if you get a dry and reasonably warm day, will help air get to the roots of your lawn.

Roses and Flowers

You can prepare seed beds for flowers by raking them over and adding compost. Mulch around roses and other flowering plants to keep the soil warm and suppress weeds.

Trees, Shrubs and Hedges

If you live in an area of heavy snowfall, your trees and shrubs might need some help. Knock snow from their branches to avoid damage. In milder climates you can do some planting! Refer to a good gardening book or website to find out what to plant when. Check to see which of these plants like compost and incorporate this when you plant them.

Vegetables, Fruit and Herbs

As soon as the ground is soft enough to work, you can catch up with any tasks that you didn't get through during the autumn and early winter. Not everyone manages to keep up with his or her garden, so just pick up wherever you can. Spend some time digging in compost, mulching or gathering leaves for leaf mould. Add anything useful to your compost heap and turn the pile to increase the heat. Rain can wash nutrients from the soil; mulching helps protect against this.

Checklist

☑ Make sure empty beds and containers are prepared in time for spring **sowing and planting**.

☑ Rejuvenate **bare patches** on your lawn in Spring by sprinkling with compost before sowing grass seed.

☑ Add any weeds from your **garden or pond** to your compost heap.

☑ Take the **last opportunity** in late spring to install water butts if you haven't done so already.

☑ Incorporate compost into **planting holes** and around new plants during spring.

☑ Summer is the ideal time for setting up a **hot (active) compost** heap.

☑ **Mulching** is important during summer to prevent water evaporation.

☑ **Late summer** is a good time to start a compost heap.

☑ Gather leaves during autumn to make **leaf mould**.

☑ **Deadheading flowers** can encourage new blooms.

☑ Keep your compost heap **insulated** during a cold winter.

☑ Keep bare ground covered with mulch to keep the **soil warm**.

☑ Make up batches of **potting mix** in mid winter.

Composting Problems & Solutions

Composting Problems

Despite your best intentions, things can go wrong with the composting process. You might end up with unwanted visitors such as wasps or rats; the compost heap might stop working or take too long to decompose. For each of these problems, there is a cause and a solution. This section is written in an A-Z format for quick reference and troubleshooting.

Ants

Ants are harmless to your compost heap and have an important role to play in the decomposition process. They help recycle plant waste and their tunnelling activities help to aerate the pile. However thousands of red ants biting you when you try to retrieve your finished compost is no laughing matter and needs to be dealt with. To eradicate ants you need to make your compost heap less attractive to them. Ants can be a particular problem during a dry, hot summer; lots of ants in your compost bin can be a sign that the pile is too dry or that you have too many browns. Check this by taking a look at your compost – is it breaking down well or is it still quite woody and dry?

Other Causes and Solutions

Ensure that your compost heap is moist enough – like a well-wrung sponge. You can water it, add some greens or, if rain is due, leave the compost heap exposed to a rain shower. Ants don't like to be disturbed, so turn the heap or aerate it while adding either water or plenty of greens such as grass clippings or fruit or vegetable peelings.

Solutions

 Make the heap **wetter** – either by watering or adding more greens.

Turn the heap to **disturb** the ants.

Beetles

Beetles are not a problem in the compost heap. They have an important role to play in the decomposition process. Smaller beetles feed on fungal spores and larger ones prey on small insects. Other species gnaw through rotting wood, which is great for your compost heap. Some beetles eat slugs, so be grateful they are in your garden!

Solutions

 No need to deal with them; they are part of a **healthy ecosystem** in your heap.

Bumblebees

In our present climate, it is a welcome site to see a nest of bumble bees. Although it might be inconvenient to have them in your compost heap, bumblebee populations have suffered massive decline in recent years and this is of great concern to conservationists. Perhaps, instead of rushing to get rid of them, you could spend a moment feeling privileged. Bumblebees are endangered and it is illegal to kill them. The best thing to do is leave them alone. They won't cause any harm to your compost heap and only 50 per cent of bees will survive the process if you try and move the nest.

They'll Soon Be Gone

Bumblebees will only take up residence in your heap until the weather cools down. When temperatures drop, the colony will die, leaving the queen free to find a different site to spend the coldest months. Bumblebees do not like to be disturbed and will often find an undisturbed compost heap to nest in. It has everything they need in terms of comfort – it's warm, moist and peaceful! The key here is to prevent them taking up residence next year by keeping your bin well aerated by turning it. This will make your heap less attractive to the bees.

Set up Another Heap

If you are desperate to continue composting, set up another heap while you are giving bed and board to your bumblebee nest. Once the cooler weather comes, the original compost heap will be all yours again!

Solutions

 Leave the bumblebees alone until temperatures drop and the colony dies.

 Start **another heap** if necessary.

 Prevent them nesting again by **aerating** the bin frequently.

Cockroaches

Like many other insects, cockroaches have their part to play in your compost heap. They eat decaying material. It's only when there are so many of them that they might move somewhere unacceptable, like your home, that you need to deal with them. Cockroaches cannot breed in hot temperatures, so ensure that your compost heap is reaching a good temperature in the middle. Turn the heap regularly to disturb the insects and cook any eggs.

Keep Them Away from the House

Try to have your compost heap away from your house – the far end of the garden is ideal. If the cockroaches decide to move on, it means that there is less of a risk that they will set up camp in your home. Make sure that you have not been adding cooked food scraps to your heap as this can attract them.

Solutions

- Keep the **temperature** up by regularly turning the heap and adding new ingredients.
- Keep the compost bin **away** from your home.
- Keep **cooked food** scraps out of your heap.

Cold Heap

If your compost pile does not heat up, it might be too small. The minimum recommended size is 1 m (3 ft) wide by 1 m (3 ft) deep and 1 m (3 ft) high to ensure that there is enough mass to retain heat. Many closed composting bins are smaller than this, but retain enough warmth as they have closed sides. Maintain the warmth of your bin by keeping the lid on and insulating in cold weather. Most of the heat, however, is generated from within the compost. A good heap will stay warm no matter what the weather.

Plenty of Nitrogen

You need good sources of nitrogen to feed the microorganisms – it is the decomposition of these raw ingredients by the microorganisms that creates heat in the pile. If your compost heap has cooled down, add some nitrogen-rich materials, such as grass clippings, mix them in and cover. As the microorganisms finish decomposing, the temperature of the heap drops. Basically, they are saying 'feed me more!' So what are you waiting for?

Oxygen

If you regularly feed your compost pile and it has still cooled down, then there might not be enough air in the heap. Aerate as you add new ingredients or on a weekly basis to introduce oxygen. The intense activity in your compost heap uses up the available oxygen and unless the pile receives more, activity will stop. Remember to add carbon-rich browns to create pockets of air throughout the pile. Make sure they are shredded finely so that decomposition can take place easily. It's all about balance – remembering to get a good C:N ratio.

Moisture

You need to keep the compost pile moist. If it has cooled down but composting has obviously not finished, it has become too dry. Grab a handful of materials from the middle of your heap and check the moisture levels. It should resemble a well-wrung sponge. If it is too dry, add some water and/or some greens, mix everything together and cover.

Insulation

In extreme weather conditions, insulate your heap with straw, plastic bubble wrap, cardboard or whatever suitable material you have. Protect the bin from cold winds and site in the sun if possible. Adding an activator such as nettles, comfrey, chicken manure or human urine can help to generate heat as well.

Solutions

 Is your open heap **large enough** to maintain heat? An open heap should be at least 1 m (3 ft) wide by 1 m (3 ft) deep and 1 m (3 ft) high.

 If you have a closed bin, keep the **lid on**.

 Insulate your bin and site it in a warm place.

 Ensure a **good C:N ratio** – add greens to increase microbial activity.

Aerate the pile and add browns to create pockets of air.

 Keep the compost **moist** – either water it or add more greens, then cover.

 Use an **activator** such as nettles, comfrey, chicken manure or human urine to kick start the decomposition process and increase heat.

Fruit Flies

Fruit flies are a common problem in compost heaps. They are not harmful – just a nuisance, and it's not very nice to get a face full of fruit flies when you open the lid. Fruit flies have an important role to play – they help to break down fruit and vegetable materials, so a few are good! Fruit flies are more prevalent during hot weather. They like humid conditions and are attracted to the sweet sugars being released from over-ripe fruits and vegetables. Unfortunately this makes most people's compost heaps in the height of summer like the best restaurant to fruit flies. They have a short lifespan, but can breed quickly in optimum conditions.

Cover Food Sources

When you add fruit or vegetable peelings to your heap, cover them with dried grass clippings or shredded paper. Ideally, you would make a hole in the middle of the compost and add the fruit peelings to the centre of the pile. Another idea is to line your kitchen caddy with newspaper and wrap everything up before taking it to the heap.

Good C:N Ratio

Ensure that you have a good C:N ratio. You need a decent amount of browns for good aeration and to attract natural predators of the fruit fly such as beetles and centipedes. By the time the seasons change and the colder months are with you, you'll find that fruit flies naturally decline in numbers.

Solutions

 Cover fruit and vegetable peelings with shredded newspaper.

 Make a **hole** in the middle of the pile and add vegetable and fruit peelings.

 Make sure the **C:N ratio** is good.

Nothing Happening

If you've dutifully been taking care of your compost and you find that nothing is happening, say, after a year or more, there are several actions you can take to rectify things. Remember a compost heap requires nitrogen, water, warmth and air. The chances are, one of these ingredients is missing.

Warmth

In a cold climate, composting can take longer. It is possible to do hot (active) composting but, if you're a beginner, the chances are you'll be cold (passive) composting. There is nothing you can do to control the weather, but you can take steps to improve conditions in your heap and to increase the heat. Insulating your heap is one way to keep heat in. Just as you would insulate your home to reduce your heating costs, you can do the same to your bin. Straw, cardboard or bubble wrap are ideal materials. Place your bin in the sunniest, warmest site of your garden if you live in a cold climate and keep it covered.

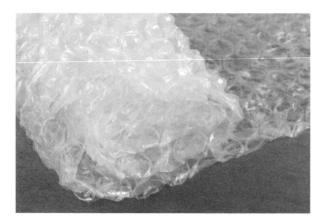

Patience

Patience is difficult for many of us. But ask yourself whether your compost is really taking a long time or if it just feels that way. Check your gardening planner and see when you started your compost heap; perhaps it hasn't been as long as you think. By taking actions to put things right, you should soon find that your compost heap starts working more quickly. Just remember to maintain all your good work and keep your heap fed, watered, warm and aired! It might take you a full year to fill your bin and then another year for it to completely cure. If you are eager to use your compost quickly, you'll need to set up two or more heaps or have a go at active composting.

Check the Progress

Before jumping to any conclusions, gather some real evidence: is your bin overflowing after you have added a year's worth of raw ingredients or is there always room for you to add new items? If there is always room, then something is happening and it is slowly rotting down. If it's overflowing, then clearly decomposition is not happening. Once you've ascertained whether or not some rotting is taking place you'll need to dig down to the bottom of the pile (or open the hatch at the bottom if you have this style of bin) and take a look. What do you see? If you see perfect compost then something good is happening, probably just not as fast as you would like.

Creepy crawlies

Your compost bin needs microorganisms, worms, insects and all sorts of other things to work properly. Are you using a system which allows these creatures in, or do you need to introduce them yourself? The best place for a compost heap is on bare soil. Heavy clay will need to be broken up before placing the bin on top of it. Grass is the next best place. If your bin does not have small holes at the bottom, it will be difficult for the necessary creatures to get in, so make sure they have access.

Aeration

Oxygen is vital to your compost heap. Try and turn the heap regularly or at least put a stick or broom handle into the centre of the pile and shake it about a bit; tumbling composters are ideal if you cannot physically manage to do this. Aerating helps to increase the heat again and get the composting process going. Having a good ratio of browns to greens in your heap creates air pockets to keep things working effectively.

Moisture

The key for moisture is having not too much, nor too little. A healthy compost heap has the texture of a well-wrung sponge. But looking at materials on the outside or top of the heap might not give you a clear indication of what is happening. Take a handful of ingredients from the centre of the pile and squeeze it. If you get a couple of drops of water from it, the moisture levels are correct. If it is dripping, you need to add more browns to soak up the excess water. If it is dry, you need to add more greens or water to your heap.

Tip

Regular attention to your compost heap should prevent most problems occuring.

Activators

Activators can be useful to give the compost heap a helping hand. Try and find a space to grow comfrey in your garden, as this is one of the best activators. Simply add a few leaves to the pile. Nettles are another great activator. If a neighbour or friend keeps chickens, try and bag some chicken manure. Fork it into your bin for one of the finest ingredients! If all else fails you can use your own activator – urine. Pour it in, mix up the heap and let nature do its work.

Solutions

- **Insulate** the heap with straw, cardboard or bubble wrap.
- Keep the compost pile in a **warm, sunny area**.
- **Patience**. Do you need to allow the compost heap more time to work?
- **Check the facts**; is there good compost in the bottom of your bin?
- Make sure there are enough **microorganisms** in your heap.
- **Aerate** the heap regularly.
- Check **moisture** levels are adequate.
- Try using an **activator** such as comfrey, nettles, chicken manure or human urine.

Rats

Many people worry about enticing rats to their compost heap. You will only get rats if they are already in the area; a compost heap does not cause rats to appear. A compost bin can be the perfect place for rats; it's quiet (rats don't like to be disturbed), warm and has a continual food supply. One common reason for finding rats in your compost is the presence of cooked food. Have you, or has another member of your household, been adding meat and fish, dairy, cooked food, bread or fatty foods to your heap? If so, you need to stop. You'll probably find that the rats will soon move to somewhere with a better menu. If the problem persists despite not adding these ingredients, experiment with omitting eggshells too.

Peace, Quiet and Warmth

Rats like peace and quiet and will run away from disturbances. Every time you walk past the compost heap, why not give it a tap or turn the contents? They'll soon find somewhere quieter to live. They also prefer a dry environment, so make sure your heap is moist in the middle. In addition, rats seek warmth and shelter. Turning the heap and maintaining a good C:N ratio will help to make conditions less favourable to rats. Rats don't like open spaces; they tend to scurry along the sides of walls, hedges and fences. If rats persist you may have to move your compost bin to a more open site.

Keep Them Out

If the bottom of your compost bin is open, you may need to take preventative measures to stop rats entering. Empty the bin and line the base with wire mesh so that access to your heap is not as easy. You'll need to use mesh with very small holes – 1 cm ($^1/_2$ in) or less, as rats can squeeze into tiny spaces. Bear in mind that rats can bite through very thin wire netting. If all else fails you might have to try a different composting system such as an enclosed tumbling one, or a food waste digester system such as a Green Cone.

Solutions

- ✓ Ensure no **cooked food** goes into your compost heap.
- ✓ **Disturb** the pile; rats like privacy.
- ✓ Keep the heap away from **fences**, **walls** and **hedges**.
- ✓ Use small **wire mesh** around the bottom of your bin.
- ✓ Try an **enclosed** composting system.

Smell of Ammonia

The smell of ammonia emanating from your compost bin is a sure sign of too much nitrogen. It can be very noticeable in the summer when lots of grass clippings are being added to the pile. Refer back to the chapter How to Compost to learn more about a C:N ratio (see page 61). Adding greens and brown is achieved by volume. For every bucket of grass clippings or vegetable peelings you add to the heap, you need to add a bucket of shredded cardboard, sawdust or woody prunings. If this is not possible, reducing the amount of grass clippings will help. Use them as mulch around plants or leave them on the grass to feed the lawn until the smell disappears from your compost heap.

Lack of Oxygen

The smell of ammonia can also be caused by the compaction of green materials and the resulting lack of oxygen, which turns the heap anaerobic. This means that the healthy microorganisms responsible for producing great compost have been replaced by those that do not need oxygen to work. Grass clippings and vegetable peelings have a habit of clumping together, excluding oxygen from the pile. Break these up with a fork and turn the pile, incorporating shredded paper if necessary. You might need to mix the pile around for a few days in a row to get the balance right and be rid of the smell.

Too Much Moisture

Too much moisture in the pile can prevent air circulating properly, which in turn can lead to the bad ammonia smell. The solution here is to ensure the heap has just the right amount of water. It needs to resemble a well-wrung sponge. If it is wetter than that, it can start to smell. If you live in a wet climate make sure that rain cannot get into your heap. Use a lid on your compost heap and keep it protected from driving rain.

Solutions

- Increase the amount of **carbon-rich browns** in the pile such as shredded cardboard and woody prunings.
- **Aerate** the pile and break up any clumps of green ingredients.
- Don't add too much **water** and protect the heap from rain.

Too Dry

If your compost heap is too dry, it will take ages to decompose. It might look as though nothing is happening at all. Composting is about taking what nature does naturally (decomposing) and providing optimum conditions to speed up the process. If you see a pile of woody branches on the forest floor protected from rainfall by a canopy of trees, the chances are you'll be seeing that heap for many years to come. However, if you take those materials and provide them with optimum conditions for decomposition the process will take less time.

HaVe YoU ThoughT Of?

Decomposition is one of nature's oldest secrets. Composting follows this example by adding favourable conditions to facilitate the process.

Vital Ingredients

When you compost at home you introduce air, warmth and moisture as well as a good balance of greens and browns to ensure a good C:N ratio. In addition, woody material is shredded as finely as possible to help the process. If your compost heap is too dry, it might be that you have put too many browns in there, that your browns are too large or that you need to add some water to the pile. Depending on the severity of dryness you can do this by watering the heap or adding some wetter greens.

Climate Considerations

If you live in a very dry, hot climate, you will need to pay more attention to getting moisture levels right. A good way to do this is to soak materials like cardboard and paper in water before adding to the heap. If your compost enclosure has a lot of air holes, then materials around the edge can dry out too quickly. A few air and drainage holes at the bottom are good, but bins with holes right up the sides don't work well in some climates. You'll need to keep turning the contents so that the outside materials reach the inside of the bin. If you live in a particularly dry, hot environment and keep experiencing dry compost you may need to line your bin, so that it is enclosed to help retain moisture. Have you left the lid off? Ensure you keep it closed except when aerating or adding new materials.

Moisture Levels and Solutions

It is far easier to rectify a heap that is too dry than one which is too wet. So if you decide to water your heap, don't go overboard. Add a little water, mix the heap, add a little more water, mix again and so on, until you reach the desired consistency. If you've added enough water the heap will warm up in a couple of days.

Solutions

 Shred browns finely and soak cardboard and paper before adding.

 Add wetter greens or water the pile.

 Line your bin if it has air holes up the side.

 Mix the **outside ingredients** into the middle of the pile.

Keep the **lid on** except when adding new ingredients or tending to your compost.

Too Hot

In some instances a compost heap can get too hot and kill off the microorganisms. If this happens, you need to wait until the pile cools and allow the ecosystem to balance itself. Too much heat is often caused by an excess of nitrogen in the pile. Add more carbon-rich materials as these create air pockets and reduce the heating effects. Aerate the pile too; this will help release any build-up of heat from the centre of the pile and reduce the overall temperature. In extreme cases, you might need to remove the ingredients from the pile and spread them out to cool down before putting them back in.

Heat Risks

In some climates, the long, hot, dry summer can lead to fire risks. They are a rare occurrence, but they do happen from time to time. Keep an eye on your heap; you may even need to site it in a cooler place during the height of the hot season. You may have to water your pile more than usual until temperatures drop. An average-sized garden compost heap is rarely a cause for concern; it is usually the really large piles that are more at risk from catching alight.

Solutions

 Aerate the pile to bring the outside ingredients into the centre or remove the contents and spread them out to cool down.

 Move the compost bin to a **cooler site**.

 Water the heap and ensure that the heap is moist throughout – not just at the edges or in the middle of the pile.

Wasps

You may find a nest of wasps in your heap. These are harmless to the compost, but unpleasant for you to have to face every time you want to add new materials. Wasps like warm, dry places with an abundance of sweet, sugary food. A compost bin in the height of warm summer containing fruit scraps is the ideal place for them! Keeping the lid on your bin should prevent them from entering in the first place, but if you have an open heap you'll have to make conditions less favourable for them.

Cover the Food

A layer of paper or dried grass clippings over any fruit waste will help dissuade the wasps. Make sure the C:N ratio is correct; lots of rotting fruit, without drier browns, is the ideal feeding place for wasps. Having said that, a wasps' nest can be a sign that your compost heap is too dry. Again, checking the C:N ratio and adding some nitrogen-rich ingredients, such as grass, or watering the heap can help.

Come out at Dusk

If you have young children and are worried about them getting stung, you might prefer to leave the infested heap alone and stop using it until the cooler weather comes. Once temperatures drop, the wasps will disappear. The good news is that wasps do not return to the same nest the following year, so you have time to take preventative measures such as checking for large air holes in your bin and sealing them up. If you want to continue using the heap despite the wasps and live in a climate where the temperature drops at night during the summer, leave the heap alone during the day and add your raw ingredients after dusk. Most wasps will have gone to bed once it's cool and the risk of getting stung is less.

Tip

Wasps are a useful predator in the garden, so try and leave them if you can.

Solutions

- **Cover fruit scraps** with layers of newspaper or dried grass clippings.
- Keep the compost heap well **covered**.
- Make sure there are no large air holes.
- **Water** the heap; a wasps' nest can be a sign that the heap is too dry.
- Add new materials to the heap **after dusk**.
- **Leave** the heap until autumn when the wasps will disappear and you can start again.
- **Aerate** frequently to disturb wasps and prevent nest building.

Wet and Slimy Compost

Wet, slimy compost is a frequent problem for many so don't panic. The most common reason for this is an imbalance of carbon and nitrogen; it is caused by too many green materials and not enough browns. A side effect of adding too many greens is that the structure of the heap tends to collapse, which closes up the air spaces. Without these everything clumps together and gets slimy.

Too Many Greens

If there are too many greens in your compost heap, the remedy is to turn the heap and add browns such as woody prunings or shredded cardboard. Too many greens can be a particular problem during the summer months when there are usually more greens available, such as grass clippings and fruit peelings. With hotter temperatures, the composting rate is faster which makes it even more important to keep the balance correct.

Store Browns

A tip for this is to find somewhere to store brown materials whenever you get them. Woody prunings can be shredded and stored in a dry place such as a shed. It's simple to keep a supply of cardboard ready to shred and add to your pile at any time. There are usually plenty of opportunities to find cardboard and paper in everyday life – toilet roll inners, egg boxes (if these cannot be reused by a supplier first), newspapers and torn up cardboard boxes for example.

Rain and Run-off

Leaving your compost bin open to the elements can result in a slimy mess. A heavy rainfall can flood the bin which not only makes it wetter, but also slows down the composting process, because it cools everything down. The solution to this is to use an enclosed compost heap and only take the lid off when adding new materials. If you are using an enclosed bin, check to see if there are drainage holes in the bottom. Sometimes compost run-off can stagnate in the bottom of the bin and make the rest of the pile too wet.

If All Else Fails

If things look really bad in your compost heap, you'll need to take quite drastic action to rescue it. Empty the bin out completely, break up any solid clumps (these are common when you put a lot of grass clippings into the compost heap) and refill the bin, using the layering technique outlined in the chapter How to Compost (see page 72).

Solutions

- Add **more browns** to the pile.
- **Aerate** the pile.
- Keep the compost protected from **rainfall** and snow.
- Ensure there are **drainage holes** at the bottom of your bin.
- Remove contents, **break them up** with a fork and refill the bin with layers of material.

PROBLEM	POSSIBLE CAUSES	SOLUTIONS
Ants	Too dry	Add more greens or water.
	Too many browns	Balance greens and browns when adding to your compost pile.
	Undisturbed heap	Disturb the ants by aerating.
Beetles	Not a problem	No need to do anything – they are part of a healthy ecosystem.
Bumblebees	Undisturbed heap	Do not disturb them – bumblebees are endangered so build another heap. Prevent them in the future with regular aeration.
Cockroaches	A few are okay	If you can only see a few then leave them.
	Heap too cold	Turn the heap to increase heat and cook cockroach eggs.
	Attracted by cooked food	Do not compost cooked food.
Heap too cold	Too small	Build a compost heap that is a minimum of 1 m (3 ft) wide, 1 m (3 ft) deep and 1 m (3 ft) high.
	Poor insulation	Keep compost bin lids closed and the sides insulated.
	Lack of nitrogen	Add more nitrogen-rich greens.
	Lack of oxygen	Aerate the pile and add shredded browns.
	Too dry	Check moisture levels and water if necessary.
	Needs activating	Add an activator such as nettles, comfrey, chicken manure or urine.

Fruit Flies	Attracted to fruit and vegetables	Cover peelings with grass clippings or newspaper.
	Lack of carbon	Add carbon-rich browns.
Nothing happening	Too cold	Keep the lid on your compost bin, insulate the sides and site in a warm place.
	Lack of patience	Composting can take time – be patient!
	Lack of microorganisms	Site compost heap on bare earth or add a spade of compost.
	Lack of air	Aerate the heap or add carbon-rich browns.
	Needs activating	Add an activator such as nettles, comfrey, chicken manure or urine.
	Too dry	Water the heap or add greens.
Rats	Undisturbed	Aerate the heap.
	Too dry	Check moisture levels and water if necessary.
	Attracted to cooked food	Do not compost cooked food.
	Easy access	Put wire around the base of your compost heap.
Smell of ammonia	Too much nitrogen	Balance nitrogen-rich greens with carbon-rich browns.
	Lack of oxygen	Turn the heap and add some browns.
	Too wet	Add more browns and keep the heap protected from the rain.
Too dry	Too many browns	Balance browns with greens for a good C:N.

Too dry	Large materials added	Shred large materials before adding.
	Not enough water	Water the heap or soak browns before using.
	Not enough greens	Add greens.
	Too many air holes	Insulate air holes up the sides of the heap, but not at the base.
	Hot, dry climate	Keep the compost covered, except when adding new material and aerating.
Too hot	Too much nitrogen	Maintain a good C:N. Don't add too many greens without browns.
	Compaction	Aerate the pile and bring the cooler, outside materials into the middle.
	Hot climate	Move your compost bin to a cooler area.
Wasps	Access	Keep compost covered.
	Attracted to food waste	Cover food with grass clippings or newspaper.
	Too dry	Water the pile and add plenty of nitrogen-rich greens.
Wet and slimy	Too much nitrogen	Ensure a good C:N by adding browns when you add greens.
	Too much water	Keep the heap protected from rain
	Compaction	Add some browns to create air pockets.
	No drainage	Ensure there are a few drainage holes at the bottom of the heap.

Checklist

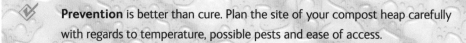

Prevention is better than cure. Plan the site of your compost heap carefully with regards to temperature, possible pests and ease of access.

Are there any **particular pests** in your vicinity? Plan how you might prevent I a problem occurring.

Do you have a **good mix** of carbon-rich and nitrogen-rich materials throughout the year? If not, decide how to rectify this.

Work out the best composting system for your **climate**.

If you have vermin problems, make sure nobody in your household is adding **cooked food** waste to the heap.

Check that your compost bin is protected from **extremes of temperature** and weather conditions.

Aerate the pile regularly to prevent many composting problems.

Plant herbs, flowers and trees in your garden that attract **beneficial insects**.

Checklist

Included here are the checklists from the end of each chapter of the book. Use them to remind yourself of what to do. Tick them off as you go along!

Why Compost?

☐ Find out what **recycling** is collected from your kerbside and use the service.

☐ Have a think about any items from your **weekly trash** that you could start to do without, reuse or recycle.

☐ Think about the amount of **fruit and vegetable peelings** you throw away – you could use them for compost.

☐ Could you **buy local** fruit and vegetables? Find out where you nearest farm shops, box schemes or orchards are and contact them.

☐ Make a goal to buy one less **bag of compost** this year and make your own instead.

☐ Get to **know your soil**; is it acid or alkaline, sandy or clay? If you know what you are dealing with, you can see your progress.

☐ Spend some time in **nature**, taking note of the cycles of life and decay.

☐ Get your **family involved**. Learn together about composting and make it an excuse to spend quality time together.

☐ Borrow a book on **organic gardening** from your library and learn about some of the benefits of an organic lifestyle.

What to Compost

☐ Write down all the things from this chapter which you **use regularly** at home so that you can see instantly what can and cannot be added to your compost pile.

☐ Instead of adding cardboard **egg boxes** to your compost pile, why not see if a local farm shop can reuse them?

☐ If you have a lot of **untreated sawdust** you could offer it to people for animal bedding.

☐ Don't add too much **paper** to your compost bin. The most ecologically sound thing to do with paper is recycle it.

☐ When you have your **hair cut** in the spring, do the birds a favour and give them some of your hair for nesting, rather than put it all in the compost bin.

☐ Even **biodegradable nappies** (diapers) cannot be composted or recycled, so why not try cloth nappies (diapers) instead?

☐ Don't add too many **textiles** to your compost heap; it's better to donate your unwanted items to a charity shop or textiles bank for reuse.

How to Compost

☐ Review the pattern between **greens and browns, carbon and nitrogen, wet and dry** ingredients so that you have a better understanding of the requirements of your compost heap.

☐ Think of an **average week** in your household – what green and brown items do you come across regularly?

☐ Decide **where to put** your compost bin – choose a sheltered spot, preferably on bare soil.

☐ Find a source of **natural activators**; do you have nettles or comfrey in your garden or a source of poultry manure? If not, your own urine is the answer!

☐ Decide how much **space and time** you can dedicate to composting and start making a plan.

☐ Start stockpiling some **useful browns** such as shredded cardboard, scrunched up newspaper and small twigs.

☐ Do you need to 'borrow' some **worms** or compost from a friend to get things started? If so, organize this.

Compost Bins & Composting Systems

☐ **Set a budget** for your compost bin and start looking at available options.

☐ Determine **what size** bin or heap you need.

☐ If you are going to make your own compost bin, start **gathering materials**.

☐ **Choose a location** for your bin – close enough to your house for filling, but convenient for where you want to use your finished compost.

☐ Look at the **pros and cons** for each type of compost bin – which one suits your needs?

☐ **How many** bins do you need? Do you have the room and the raw materials for them?

☐ Do you need to look at **smaller options** such as a wormery or a bokashi bin?

Other Types of Composting

☐ Consider the other methods of composting outlined in this chapter – is there one that **suits your lifestyle**?

☐ If you have trees in your garden, why not make **leaf mould** this year?

☐ Would a **Green Cone** or **Green Johanna** be better for your needs? Do you have the right location for one? A Green Johanna needs shade and a Green Cone needs full sun.

☐ Do you need to compost **garden waste**? If so, you'll need a Green Johanna.

☐ If you need an **indoor composting** method, look at the types of kitchen waste you create most of – fruit and vegetable peelings are better for a wormery, cooked food waste is better dealt with by a bokashi bin.

☐ Find out the **prices** of different wormeries and choose the best one for your household.

☐ Remember that a bokashi bin requires special **effective microorganisms**; shop around for the best deal.

☐ If you decide on a **bokashi bin**; do you have somewhere to deposit the finished contents?

Using Compost

☐ Check which of your plants **love compost** and which ones don't in a good gardening book or website.

☐ Keep a little of your finished compost back for starting a **new batch**.

☐ How much compost have you made? You might need to **prioritize** where you use it, focusing on neglected soil first.

☐ Remember that you are **feeding the soil**, not the plants. Healthy soil produces healthy plants.

☐ **Apply mulches** around established trees and shrubs in a 3–8 cm (1–3 in) layer.

☐ **Water plants** thoroughly before mulching, apply the mulch and then water again.

☐ Put a handful of compost into **transplanting holes** and around new plants.

☐ Before using up all your compost, make a batch of **compost tea** to use as a foliar feed.

☐ Where you can buy **horticultural sand**? Shop around for a good deal if you want to make your own potting compost.

☐ Sprinkle some compost **over your grass** for a green and lush lawn.

The Composting Year

- [ ] Make sure beds and containers are prepared for spring **sowing and planting**.

- [ ] Incorporate compost into **planting holes** and around new plants during spring.

- [ ] Summer is the ideal time for setting up a **hot (active) compost** heap.

- [ ] **Mulching** is important during summer to prevent water evaporation.

- [ ] Gather leaves during autumn to make **leaf mould**.

- [ ] Keep your compost heap **insulated** during a cold winter.

- [ ] Keep bare ground covered with mulch to keep the **soil warm**.

Composting Problems & Solutions

- [ ] **Prevention** is better than cure. Plan the site of your compost heap carefully with regards to temperature, possible pests and ease of access.

- [ ] Are there any **particular pests** in your vicinity? Plan how you might prevent a problem occurring.

- [ ] Do you have a **good mix** of carbon-rich and nitrogen-rich materials throughout the year? If not, decide how to rectify this.

- [ ] Work out the best composting system for your **climate**.

- [ ] If you have vermin problems, make sure nobody in your household is adding **cooked food** waste to the heap.

- [ ] Check that your compost bin protected from **extremes of temperature** and weather conditions.

- [ ] **Aerate the pile** regularly to prevent many composting problems.

Further Reading

Appelhof, M., *Worms Eat My Garbage*, Flower Press, 1997

Callard, S. and Millis, D., *The Complete Book of Green Living: A Practical Guide to Eco-friendly Living*, Andre Deutsch Ltd, 2001

Campbell, S., *Let it Rot!: The Gardener's Guide to Composting*, Storey Publishing, 1998

Constantino, M., *Living Green*, Flame Tree Publishing, 2009

Ebeling, E., *Basic Composting: All the Skills and Tools You Need to Get Started*, Stackpole Books, 2003

Foster, C., *Compost*, Cassell Illustrated, 2005

Gow McDilda, D., *365 Ways to Live Green*, Adams Media, 2008

Guerra, M., *The Edible Container Garden: Fresh Food from Tiny Spaces*, Gaia Books Ltd, 2000

Harrison, J., *Vegetable Growing Month By Month*, Right Way, 2008

Hegarty, M., *The Little Book of Living Green*, Nightingale Press, 2007

Hessayon, D. G., *Vegetable and Herb Expert*, Expert Books, 2007

Koontz, R. M., *Composting: Nature's Recyclers*, Picture Window Books, 2002

Nancarrow, L. and Taylor, J. H., *The Worm Book: The Complete Guide to Worms In Your Garden*, Ten Speed Press, 1998

Noyes, N., *Easy Composters You Can Build*, Storey Publishing, 1995

Oster, D. and Walliser, J., *Grow Organic: Over 250 Tips and Ideas for Growing Flowers, Veggies, Lawns and More*, St. Lynns Press, 2007

Pears, P., *Create Compost*, Impact Publishing Ltd, 2007

Pears, P., *All About Compost: Recycling Household and Garden Waste*, Search Press Ltd, 1999

Pilkington, G., *Composting With Worms: Why Waste Your Waste*, Eco-Logic Books, 2005

Pleasant, B. and Martin, D. L., *The Complete Compost Gardening Guide*, Storey Publishing, 2008

Purnell, B., *Crops in Pots: 50 Great Container Projects Using Vegetables, Fruit and Herbs*, Hamlyn, 2007

Scott, N., *Composting: An Easy Household Guide*, Green Books, 2006

Scott, N., *Reduce, Reuse, Recycle: An Easy Household Guide*, Green Books, 2004

Spence, I., *Gardening Month by Month*, Dorling Kindersley, 2007

Strauss, R., *Self Sufficiency: Household Cleaning*, New Holland Publishers, 2009

Thompson, K., *Compost: The Natural Way to Make Food for Your Garden*, Dorling Kindersley, 2007

Winch, T. and Seton, H., *How to 'Cook' Compost*, The National Trust, 2008

Websites

www.communitycompost.org
Promoting and supporting community composting in the UK with practical advice on setting up your own scheme.

www.compost.org
The Composting Council of Canada is the central resource and network for the composting industry in Canada.

www.compostingcouncil.org
US Composting Council which funds research, runs events and publishes resources on composting.

www.compostthis.co.uk
List of what can and can't be composted and why and tips for adding to your compost heap.

www.freecycle.org
Keep stuff out of the landfill by giving and getting items for free. A great place to source and gift unwanted pallets, water butts and compost bins.

www.garden.org
US National Gardening Association website offering general information, expert advice, publications, lessons and grants.

www.gardenguides.com
Online gardening information on plants, pests, gardening tips and techniques and more.

www.gardenorganic.org.uk
The British national charity for organic growing with lots of information on composting and gardening all year round.

www.howtocompost.org
Provides composting information and links to other people involved in all forms of composting.

http://myzerowaste.com
The Green family's blog about reducing the amount of waste they send to landfill each week.

www.recyclenow.com/compost
Good basic information about composting and the chance to buy a subsidized bin in the UK.

www.rhs.org.uk
Royal Horticultural Society website including gardening and composting advice.

www.self-sufficient.co.uk
Wide range of information about self-sufficient living.

www.sgaonline.org.au
Sustainable Gardening Australia; lots of sustainable gardening information delivered free to your inbox.

www.the-organic-gardener.com
Lots of practical tips about composting and reviews of different composting systems.

www.zerowastewa.com.au/organics
Supports the wise use of organic resources that would otherwise be considered to be waste.

Index